ENTERTAINMENT LAW

IN A NUTSHELL

By

SHERRI L. BURR

Professor of Law

University of New Mexico

THOMSON

™

WEST

Mat # 40279809

© 2004 West, a Thomson business
     610 Opperman Drive
     P.O. Box 64526
     St. Paul, MN 55164–0526
     1–800–328–9352

ISBN 0–314–15516–3

TEXT IS PRINTED ON 10% POST
CONSUMER RECYCLED PAPER

In memory of the
Hon. Thomas Tang
U.S. Circuit Judge
Ninth Circuit Court of Appeals
(1922-1995)

ACKNOWLEDGEMENTS

This book is dedicated to the Honorable Thomas Tang, for whom I clerked from 1985-86 when he served on the Ninth Circuit Court of Appeals. Judge Tang was a tireless devotee to the cause of justice and it was my privilege to study with him for the year following my graduation from law school.

The author thanks the following people who have given interviews over the years to assist with her entertainment law related research: Wally Amos, Diane Bloom, Greg Brooker, Johnnie Cochran, Max Evans, Chris Eyre, Guillermo Figueroa, Stephen Frears, John Carlos Frey, Walon Green, Bob Guiney, Tony Hillerman, Matt Jackson, Jonathon Miller, Shirley MacLaine, Jon Moritsugu, Duncan North, Keali'i Reichel, Jim Rogers, Sam Wong, and Frank Zuniga.

Several people have assisted me with the formatting and proofreading of this manuscript and I now thank them. Karen Talley searched the web for the Century Schoolbook font. She and Joseph Blecha helped me set up the manuscript to conform to the publisher's specifications. Barbara Jacques prepared the table of cases. I also appreciate the time generosity of the following individuals for proofreading at least one chapter of this book: Krista Allen, Patty Allred, Joseph Blecha, Janet Cox, E.J. Fenoglio, Fred Hart, Kathleen Hessler, Barbara Jacques, Kay Lamb, Sue Mann, Jeane McKenna, Jonathon Miller, Awadagin Pratt, and Susan Wyatt. A special thanks goes to Sue Mann and Jonathan Miller for reviewing the entire manuscript. Thank you all.

OUTLINE

TABLE OF CASES

References are to Pages

A

B

C

D

E

F

G

H

I

K

L

M

N

O

P

R

Y

Z

ENTERTAINMENT LAW

IN A NUTSHELL

"It's nice to be cited in a law book and not be a suspect."

Tony Hillerman, Author
Skinwalkers, A Thief of Time

INTRODUCTION

Hollywood is a place, but more importantly an industry based in Los Angeles with national offshoots in New York and Nashville, and global components around the world. The entertainment business is central to the lives of most Americans and to the United States economy. According to Variety Magazine, entertainment recently supplanted food as this country's greatest export. *See* Susan Crabtree, *Casting Against Type*, Variety.com, July 1, 2004. Because of the ubiquitous nature of the entertainment exports, other countries are routinely exposed to U.S. culture. Their citizens often seek to emulate what they see on big and small screens, what they hear on the radio or their compact disk players, or what they read.

The many players within the entertainment business rely on the law and lawyers to look after their interests. Lawyers who do not understand how the entertainment business works are at a distinct disadvantage when it comes to protecting their clients. It is not enough for a lawyer to read a contract and advise clients on its meaning if he does not understand the intricacies of the agreement's special meanings. Clients come to lawyers seeking advice on seemingly incomprehensible legal language. Many smart lawyers make assumptions about entertainment related issues that are wrong. As a consequence, they bring misfortune to their clients and sometimes themselves.

Similarly, numerous talented individuals have become so thrilled when a Hollywood person comes knocking on their door that they unwittingly sign anything placed before them. By reading this book, film artists, television talent, musicians, and other creators will appreciate the value of consulting well-versed attorneys before signing on the dotted line.

Because of this necessity to understand how the entertainment business works in order to comprehend the law that applies to it, this book's first three chapters provide an overview of the film, television, and music industries. Chapters 1 – 3 discuss the process of creating film, television, and music products, as well as the major players who have different interests. These chapters also converse about particularized components of the three businesses.

Chapter 4 scrutinizes the efforts of entertainers to protect their products from censorship. Entertainers have had their free speech rights curtailed for political reasons, as during the McCarthy era. Other entertainment products have been accused of touting obscenity, which does not enjoy the protection of the First Amendment. Still other creative output has been labeled excessively violent and charged as contributing to the tortious and violent behavior of third parties.

Chapter 4 explores censoring efforts that have succeeded and failed. It demonstrates that censorship brings more attention and often more resources to the author(s) of the sought to be banned articles. Indeed, film and other artists have come to relish the attention as patrons line up to see films others tell them they shouldn't see or to buy music that a certain group has told them to avoid.

Chapter 5 highlights intellectual property law by revealing how the laws of ideas, copyrights, trademarks, patents, and trade secrets protect products like films, games, music, television shows, theater plays, and books. Over the decades, fiction authors have accidentally lost the rights to their characters or have found themselves in legal quicksand by producing material based on the copyrighted characters of other professionals. This chapter discusses not only how to protect all authors' works, but also details the elements of infringement cases. Chapter 5 provides a synopsis of several problematic cases.

Chapter 6 focuses on representing entertainers, particularly the importance of agents, managers, lawyers, and unions to the successful career. Talented individuals sometimes find themselves in a paradox. When they need assistance they can't get it, and to obtain aid requires a certain level of verifiable talent. Chapter 6 describes some of the legal issues involved in acquiring representation.

Chapter 7 discusses the issues involved in the relationship between credits and compensation. Credits acknowledge the contribution of the talented individual to the particular project. An individual's compensation increases with the success of the projects attributed to him. Thus talent and their attorneys need to understand the nature of credits, how they are acquired, and their links to receiving revenue. In the film and television industry, for example, contracts often contain references to guaranteed, deferred, and contingent compensation. Many talented individuals misunderstand these terms to their regret as they watch the hit they helped create generate hundreds of millions of dollars in profits for others and nothing more for themselves beyond the revenue that was initially guaranteed to them. Chapter 7 also contains information important to musicians.

Chapter 8 analyzes different types of contracts and their peculiarities in the entertainment industry, including some of the fine points that make them similar yet different. Film and television contracts, for example, include clauses that are set by union regulation, whereas music contracts for most bands do not. The exceptions are symphony orchestra contracts negotiated between the American Federation of Musicians and the management of the orchestra. Even so, classical musicians have watched their earnings barely keep up with inflation as conductor and management salaries skyrocket.

Between reading chapters 6 and 8, the attorney should understand the difference between what talent has already obtained through union negotiated agreements and what can still be bargained for. The distinction is critical so that talent and their lawyers do not waste energy and time asking for items, like breaks, that the individual already has, and concentrates on augmenting the minimum pay and other perks to make the talent's life more bearable on set or on stage.

Chapter 9 covers issues associated with celebrity status. An individual may attain this right of passage through sheer force of enormous ability or due to notoriety associated with infamous behavior. Either way, the newfound celebrity status can be exploited to generate additional revenue for the individual. This chapter discusses the advantages and disadvantages to possessing celebrity status, including the actions of ordinary folks and the media that lead to violations of the entertainer's right to privacy. Celebrities may also exploit their right to publicity. This recently developed form of intellectual property permits entertainers and sports stars to profit commercially from the popularity of their names and images.

Chapter 9 also discusses estate planning, which has gained in importance because many entertainers make more money after their deaths than they did during while alive. This enables them to ably support family members left behind or to create charitable institutions to impact social concerns that they cared about during their lifetimes. Chapter 9 reviews the legal issues associated with dying intestate, i.e. without a will, or testate, i.e., with a will. It also reviews issues associated with creating trusts.

This book concludes with a discussion of the globalization of the entertainment industry and the changes that have taken place as producers seek to create products that cross cultural boundaries in the international marketplace. Film and television industries have arisen in countries throughout the world, along with unique musical sounds. This globalization process means more Americans have been exposed to Indian weddings and Brazilian music and vice versa. Chapter 10 examines global piracy of entertainment products, the internationalization of entertainment production, and the availability of appropriate legal forums to hear disputes between nationals of different countries.

This book covers all of the above and more. As *American Idol* judges say to successful television contestants, "Welcome to Hollywood."

CHAPTER 1

THE FILM INDUSTRY

The film industry comprises a vibrant component of the entertainment industry. On a weekly basis, millions of individuals in the United States and abroad flock to view the products produced in Hollywood. During 2004's weekend #27 (July 1-4), for example, Hollywood studios sold $223,258,510 in movie tickets within the United States alone.

The business of Tinseltown can be amazing and exciting as talented people seek to fulfill their dreams. The goal of legal practitioners is to keep aspirations from turning into nightmares.

A. THE FILM PROCESS

The film process begins with a pitch. Agents, managers, actors, and producers routinely make brief presentations on their projects to people in a position to provide resources or ultimately "green-light" the film. Green-light is an industry term referring to the ability of someone with power to give the final approval to send the movie into production.

Typically, producers will be accorded three minutes and writers will receive 45 minutes to pitch their ideas. The writer is expected to outline the story, including the beginning, middle and end. She should be able to provide character and story arcs, indicating how both the main character and the overall plot will develop.

Immediately following the pitch meeting, a writer might turn over the entire script and a producer will prepare and submit a treatment if there is sufficient interest A treatment can range from a page or two to several dozen pages. The treatment provides an overview of the film, including plotlines, essential characters, sometimes locations and settings, and an estimate of what it would take to make the movie work financially. The purpose of the treatment is to give the reader a sense of how this project might develop on screen and sometimes the cost.

This pre-production process also involves preparing and submitting scripts, hiring talent (actors and directors) and the production crew, scouting locations, and obtaining financing. Some directors may rehearse their actors during this phase. This gives them a sense of the emotional development of their characters because the movie will be shot out of sequence. Location availability, weather, and other variables determine the order of production. The ending could be shot before the middle and thus the actor must be prepared to emotionally deliver where the character is at that stage.

With all aspects of pre-production settled, the film moves into the production phase during which principal photography commences and the movie is shot. The production supervisor prepares daily call sheets to indicate which scene will be shot on a particular day and which actors and technicians are expected to be on set. The call sheets also indicate arrival times.

Post-production encompasses editing and putting together all the pieces of the film, including dialogue and soundtracks. Sidney Lumet, the director of over 40 films including *12 Angry Men, The Verdict*, and *Serpico*, describes the mix as the only dull part of moviemaking. With this component, the filmmakers put all the sound tracks together to make the final sound track of the movie, SIDNEY LUMET, MAKING MOVIES 186 (1995). The last stage is to color balance the film and produce the answer print, which will be used to print the film shown in theaters.

Since anything can go wrong in the pre-production, production, and post production phases, it is important for lawyers to have a sense of the overall process, as well as the players and the types of films.

B. THE PLAYERS

Filming is a collaborative enterprise, requiring the aid of many individuals and groups to bring a final product to completion. The film then goes theatre where an audience can view it. Some films deemed un-commercial for theaters may go straight to video. Others may be played on airlines. Many more will ultimately receive cable, satellite, network television broadcasts.

Several players contribute to the final product and their roles are discussed in turn.

1. SCREENWRITERS

Writers often launch the film process. Writers may be inspired to craft a screenplay from an original idea or a producer may bring them a book or theatrical play and ask them to adapt it for the big screen. Walon Green, who received an Oscar nomination for *The Wild Bunch* and is credited with 13 feature films, says, "[t]he first obligation a writer has is to make sure he's not going to be sued, that he didn't steal the idea from someone." [1]

Greg Brooker, who received co-credit for writing *Stuart Little* with M. Night Shyamalan, says, "A lot of writers can make a good living

---

[1] BURR & HENSLEE, ENTERTAINMENT LAW: CASES AND MATERIALS IN FILM, TELEVISION, AND MUSIC 19 (2004).

writing screenplays in Hollywood, even if they [the screenplays] don't see the light of day. *Id.* at 165. Brooker added, "Writers tend to keep on the periphery of the business. You don't see a lot of writers hanging out at parties because they're home writing." *Id.*

In *Separation of Rights for Screen and Television Writers*, L.A. LAWYER (2001), Grace Reiner, discuses the most recent addition to the separated rights possessed by writers--the right of reacquisition. Reiner ways the writer has the right to buy back original material not based on any preexisting material that has not been produced within five years. She says that [th]e writer may do so as long as the material is not in active development.... To reacquire the material, the writer must pay the company the amount the writer was paid for the purchase and/or writing services." Further, Reiner writes that the writer must obligate the new buyer to pay the balance of direct literary material costs plus interest, which is "due upon commencement of principal photography." *Id.*

2. PRODUCERS

The general public may not recognize producers, who are most visible at the annual Academy Awards ceremony as they are the individuals who collect the Oscar® for Best Picture. In her book, *Hello, He Lied*, Lynda Obst says producers "breathe life into [a] movie—from its infancy as [an article or book] through its adolescence as a script being written against a

tight time clock, and finally into its adulthood—
by finding a director and choosing and securing
the cast." LYNDA OBST, HELLO, HE LIED 5 (1996).
She describes the greatest crisis for a producer
as "the threat of watching your baby die." *Id.*

In *Blaustine v. Burton*, 9 Cal. App. 3d 161,
88 Cal. Rptr. 319 (Cal. App. 1970), the
functions of a motion picture producer like Obst
were described as follows:

> (1) Generate the enthusiasm of the various
> creative elements as well as to bring them
> together;
> (2) Search out variable locations which
> would be proper for the artistic side of the
> production and would be proper from the
> logistical physical production side;
> (3) create a budget that would be acceptable
> from the physical point of view as well as
> satisfactory from the point of view of
> implementing the requirements of the script;
> (4) m ake arrangements with foreign
> government[s] where photography would
> take place;
> (5) supervise the execution of the script, the
> implementation of it onto film;
> (6) supervise the editing of all the
> production work down through the dubbing
> process and the release printing process, at
> least through the answer print process with
> Technicolor ...;
> (7) the obligation of consulting with the
> [studio] people on advertising and publicity;
> (8) arrange casting;

(9) engage the interest of the kind of star or stars that they [the studio people] would find sufficiently attractive to justify an investment; and

(10) develop the interest of a proper director.

Id. at 167. Those are the roles that the main producer must take on during the preproduction and production process.

Producers are with the project from beginning to end. Their job is usually to set the wheels in motion with an idea or a book and then hire the talent and secure financing. This can be a chicken and egg process as the bigger the name of the talent, the easier it is for producers to secure financing and to sell various foreign and ancillary rights to the film. While some producers operate on the word of the individuals, many more obtain written agreements to lock in talent to a particular project to be produced at a specified time.

Even before the film is completed, producers must also secure domestic and foreign box office distribution. They also seek to sell the film for viewing on airplanes, cable, satellite, and broadcast television, DVD and VHS tapes, and to turn characters from the film into merchandise available for purchase in stores. In other words, the producer must take advantage of all the revenue sources that a film can generate.

3. DIRECTORS

Directors are responsible for the entire look and feel of the physical product. Sidney Lumet, the director of dozens of films, calls what he does "the best job in the world." SIDNEY LUMET, MAKING MOVIES 3 (1995). Depending on how complicated is the physical production of the movie, he is in preproduction "anywhere from two and a half to six months. And, depending on how much work had to be done on the script, perhaps for months before preproduction began.... There are no minor decisions in movie making." *Id.* at 7.

In describing his contributions to *Dr. Zhivago*, David Lean said he works with the writer to obtain an acceptable shooting script, rehearses the writers, and gives direction to the cameraman, set designer, costume designer, sound men, editor, composer, and even the laboratory that prepares the final print. *See* Marc Caro, *The Director or the Writer: Whose Film is It?*, CHICAGO TRIBUNE, Nov. 24, 2000.

Independent directors of small budget films can be involved in raising money, luring talent, securing gun permits, enforcing child labor laws, and negotiating with film commissions. John Carlos Frey, the director of *The Gatekeeper*, shot his film in 18 days at a cost of $200,000. To do so, he says, required that "the actors work for nearly free, the crew works nearly for free, your locations get donated, your food gets donated, and you go begging, basically, to pull it off." Burr and Henslee, *supra* note 1, at 243. Frey financed his film by taking out a second mortgage on his home, borrowing from family members, draining his savings account, and running up credit card debt. Frey says he attracted an award-winning Australian cinematographer who was "dying to get a U.S. film credit." *Id.*

After casting a child actor in a major role, Frey familiarized himself with child labor laws, which limit the hours that a child can work and labor union laws that regulate adult hours. He even needed to secure gun permits for the fake guns in the film, in case police officers drove by. When he needed to blow up a building, he contacted the San Diego Film commission, which ran interference between him and fire department. For all this trouble, Frey made "a story very close to his heart," which won numerous awards at independent film festivals. *Id.* at 244-245.

Another director of independent films, John Moritsugu, also makes movies about things that matter to him. He says, "[f]rom the time you start to the time you finish, it can take up to five or ten years to make a movie.... With   my movies, I have a voice in society. It gives me a chance to put a little bit of my money and all of my time and [all] of my friends' time and energy into a project that ... ultimately will ... say something and will hopefully affect something." *Id.* at 245. Moritsugu says he directed the 1999 *Fame Whore* to call attention to "people who seek fame at any cost.... There is a naïve view that once you're famous, that everything will fall into place. Fame can be a particularly deadly drug." *Id.*

4. ACTORS

For actors, fame accompanies stardom and super stardom. Prior to that time, many attend fine arts colleges and independent film classes to hone their craft. Actors give physical embodiment to the writer's words and the director's instructions. They may find work in film, television, music videos, and theatrical plays.

Stars are actors who have reached a certain level of recognition in their profession. William Goldman describes a star as "whoever *one* studio executive with 'go' power *thinks* is a star and will underwrite with a start date."[2] Goldman defines a superstar as "someone they'll all kill for." *Id.* Stars and superstars provide the shorthand for a picture as industry insiders may pitch a "Bruce Willis action flick" or a "Wayans Brother comedy" to studio executives seeking financing for their film. Because star names are instantly recognizable, producers have an easier time raising revenue if stars or superstars are attached to their pictures.

---

[2] WILLIAM GOLDMAN, ADVENTURES IN THE SCREEN TRADE 13 (1983).

Stars come and go with the popularity of their films. Goldman says an actor reaches stardom invariably by mistakes committed when another name that is a bigger box office draw passes on a picture that became the breakthrough hit for the successor actor. *Id.* at 13-14. For examples, he cites how Montgomery Clift turned down "the William Holden part in *Sunset Boulevard*, the James Dean part in *East of Eden*, the Paul Newman part in *Somebody Up There Likes Me*, and the [Marlon] Brando part in *On the Waterfront*." *Id.* at 14. These roles all helped these gentlemen become stars, and for Marlon Brandon won him his first Oscar for Best Actor. Actress Shirley MacLaine was discovered on Broadway when as an understudy she took over after the lead broke her leg. Burr and Henslee, *supra* note 1, at 258.

Actors are essential to over 95% of film products. Even animated films that are put together with illustrators and computers hire actors to lend their voices to fictional characters. Brad Pitt, for example, voiced the animated character Sinbad in the 2003 film by the same name, and physically embodied the Greek mythical hero Achilles in the 2004 *Troy.* With the advent of technological change, some computers can generate characters that look alive and someday could replace real actors, but that day seems well into the future.

5. TECHNICAL STAFF

The technical staff makes the production work. They are involved in preproduction process and once the production begins, several are on location before the actors arrive, setting up the set and the lights. Editors fashion raw footage into a understandable product during post-production.

The art director is responsible for the overall look and feel of the set. Art directors can make a picture feel as luminous as a painting by an old master, as Christina Schaffer achieved with the 2003 *Girl with a Pearl Earring,* or as an impressionist canvas, as Thomas Voth and Christian Wintter accomplished with the 1998 *What Dreams May Come.*

The costume designer creates the clothes that the actors wear. Edith Head was nominated for 35 Oscars between 1948 and 1977 for best costume design. She won so many times that Director John Huston once joked that an Academy Award was written into her contract. *See* Walter Scott's Personality Parade, PARADE MAGAZINE, June 27, 2004, at 2.

The makeup director creates the looks of the character. Lee Grimes and Toni G. turned Charlize Theron, an actress noted for her beauty, into an unattractive serial killer for her feature role as Aileen Wuornos in *Monster.* Makeup artists have also been known to transform men into women, as when Robin

Williams played Mrs. Doubtfire in a film by the same name, and two African-American men Marlon and Shawn Wayans, became Caucasian females for the 2004 *White Chicks*.

The director of cinematography is responsible for capturing the entire film process in moving imagery. Freddie Francis captured the Academy Award for best cinematography by photographing a gritty and realistic vision of the horrors of the Civil War from the perspective of black soldiers who fought on the side of the North. An excellent cinematographer can make or break an epic adventure whose story sweeps the audience along.

Gaffers are the lighting technicians who bestow ambiance on the set. By appropriately illuminating the actors, gaffers create mood and can make the talent look older or younger as the situation may require.

Teamsters drive the actors and crew material from location to location. Production Assistants are usually recent college graduates who do whatever is needed, from making coffee, picking up dry cleaning to chaperoning visitors to the set.

Editors are a critical to the post-production process as they take the raw footage and turn it into a story. Certain types of films, like documentaries, can be "editorial intense," requiring an editor to pull together the story line. *See* Author Interview with Craig Serling, Burr and Henslee, *supra* note 1, at 318.

The music composer creates the score. At the Academy Award ceremonies, they frequently show composers working on a keyboard as the movie plays on a screen. The job of the composer is to match the mood the director is trying to depict on screen. A good score can foreshadow dread or foretell a happy ending.

These are only a few of the many talented individuals who lend their expertise to the making of a film. Their positions and names scroll down the screen at the end of the picture. Depending on the type of picture, such as with an action flick, the names of those who created special effects may be listed. For his 2004 documentary *Fahrenheit 911*, Michael Moore listed all his production assistants, interns, and law firms who contributed to his film.

6. STUDIOS

Studios are corporations with the power and the resources to underwrite a film. Goldman describes studio executives as ex-agents, who "are intelligent, brutally overworked men and women who share one thing in common with baseball managers: They wake up every morning of the world with the knowledge that sooner or later they're going to get fired." Goldman, *supra* note 2, at 39. The reason for this, Goldman says is that in Hollywood, "Nobody Knows Anything." *Id.* Because they can never predict "what's going to work," Goldman maintains that every time out is a guess—and if they're lucky, "an educated one." *Id.*

More recently, the agents who have transferred over to become studio executives include Michael Ovitz and Ron Meyer who created CAA, Creative Artist Agency. Ovitz spent 14 months at Disney before parachuting out with $140 million, the equivalent of nearly 10 percent of Disney's earnings in 1996. In 1995, Meyer began a more successful and longer tenure as the head of Universal Studios. The role of agents will be discussed in more detail in Chapter 6.

Nevertheless, studio executives are the individuals with the power to make the picture a go. For producers, directors, actors, and crew, that is perhaps the ultimate clout.

C. FILM TYPES

Unlike books, where nonfiction works far outnumber fiction, films are predominantly fictional. Even when based on a true story, components will be fictionalized such as the composite characters in the film *Amadeus*, about the life of classical composer and musician Mozart. Films may be dramatic, comical, or musical. *Amadeus* featured all the above, although it was not a full scale musical like the adaptations of Broadway musicals *The Sound of Music* or *Chicago*, which both took home Oscars for best picture in 1965 and 2002 respectively.

Action films are highly sought after by studios as they are most likely to generate gold at the box office and through subsidiary sales, even though they are expensive and dangerous to make. Several action films have brought death to the set. Special effects caused a helicopter to crash on the set of *Twilight Zone: The Movie*, killing actor Vic Morrow and two children. The director John Landis was charged with involuntary manslaughter, although he was eventually acquitted. On the set of *The Crow*, a real bullet was loaded into a gun and used to shoot actor Brandon Lee. His father, Hong Kong action star Bruce Lee, also met an untimely death.

Action films can be based on comic book heroes, such as *Batman, Spiderman*, or *Superman*, or on best-selling fantasy books like the *Harry Potter* series. They may be characters created from a writer's imagination, such as *Rambo* or *Rocky*. Action films are likely to be seen over and over again by 25-year-old or younger males, who comprise the biggest segment of the film-purchasing audience.

Titanic, a romantic drama based on a renowned tragedy, was the first film to make nearly $2 billion dollars in revenue at the box office and the first to become a hit due to 25-year-old and younger females purchasing repeat tickets.

Studios also like action films because they travel well to foreign countries and translate easily into different languages. Action films need less dialogue to make them understood by the audience and are less culturally nuanced. In contrast, comedies generate most of their revenue in the country of origin where the audience more easily understands the jokes.

Many animated films become blockbusters for studios. *Beauty and the Beast*, *Shrek*, and *Finding Nemo* respectively spawned over $100, $200, and $300 million in box office ticket sales. Disney was initially the king of animated films with classics such as *Snow White* and *The Lion King*, but other studios, such as Pixar Studios and Dreamworks, have successfully released animated films. They are less expensive to make, and yet they resonate with kids who beg their parents to take them to the theater and later purchase the DVD or video version of the film, along with all kinds of character merchandize. While Broadway has long been a source of inspiration for films, it is only recently that films, such as *Beauty and the Beast* and *The Lion King* have been turned into theatrical hits.

Documentaries supply an up and coming art form. They are the film equivalent of nonfiction books. As their production costs declines and their box office value increases, they are more likely to be financed and distributed as feature films.

Morgan Spurlock's *Super Size Me*, which chronicles the effects of a 30-day McDonald's diet on the director's health, cost $65,000 to create and yet became a top-10 film while screening on 230 screens, barely 6% of the 3855 screens reserved for 2004 blockbuster *Harry Potter and the Prisoner of Azkaban*. After 73 days in U.S. movie theaters, *Super Size Me* had taken in $10,633,019.[3]

Perhaps the best indication of a film's impact is the response. When *Super Size Me* opened in Australia to the best documentary debut in that country's history, McDonald's Australia countered with an advertising campaign to discredit Spurlock's action of eating three meals at McDonald's for 30 days as "stupid." [4]

Filmmaker Michael Moore's 2002 documentary *Bowling for Columbine* made over $21.3 million at the box office while at its height playing to approximately 230 theaters. *Bowling for Columbine* set a box office record for documentaries until Moore released *Fahrenheit*

---

[3] VARIETY WEEKLY BOX OFFICE, Jul. 16-18, 2004, *available at* http://www.variety.com/index.asp?layout=b_o_weekend_all&dept=Film&sort=BOLASTWEEKEND

[4] Stephen Dabkowski, *Spitting chips, McDonald's fights back*, THE AGE, available at http://www.theage.com.au/articles/2004/06/13/1087065034025.html.

911 on June 25, 2004. The latter film cost $6 million to make and $10 million to distribute yet generated $21.8 million in domestic ticket revenue during its first weekend and $38.9 million throughout its first week at the box office. *Fahrenheit 911* opened at 868 theaters, a record number of engagements for a documentary, and expanded to twice as many theaters on July 2, 2004. The controversial nature of *Farhenheit* 911 will be discussed in Chapter 4, which addresses the topic of censorship.

The successes of Spurlock and Moore may lead to the production and distribution of more feature length documentaries. For newcomers to the film industry, documentaries can be a great way to begin, but they are not without their headaches.

Diane Bloom, who possesses a PhD in psychology, made her first documentary without ever talking to a lawyer. *An Unlikely Friendship* uncovers an amiable relationship that developed between a black female civil rights activist and the leader of the Durham, North Carolina, Ku Klux Klan. Bloom did not obtain release agreements from her subjects, the person she retained to host the documentary, or those who provided equipment. Once the film became a hit, several individuals came forward and claimed an ownership interest in the film. She said afterwards, "I would [now] hire a lawyer at the beginning. I could have saved myself a lot of grief." Burr and Henslee, *supra* note 1, at 49.

Shorts furnish another form of filmmaking. Screenwriter Greg Brooker made *Nosferatu L.A.-02*, a story that imagines Dracula coming to live in Los Angeles and experiencing loneliness as people react to his appearance, to become his "calling card to get directing work." *Id.* at 166. Shorts, which can range in screen time from 5 to 30 minutes, are often displayed in groups at film festivals or at a theater.

CHAPTER 2

THE TELEVISION INDUSTRY

The first television set was invented in the 1920s. It consisted of a small screen (anywhere from three to twelve inches wide diagonally) inside a big box[5] displaying black and white imagery when plugged in and turned on. Programming was limited at a time when radio was the most popular form of entertainment. It wasn't until the 1950s that television came into its own as a popular media, helped along by the popularity of *I Love Lucy*. Currently, a television set can be found in approximately 90% of American homes, and it is the most popular form of entertainment for many.

This chapter explores the legal issues involved in the television industry. The chapter begins by discussing the television process of creating a show from an idea. It then addresses television cultural issues related to society and diversity, and the rise of cable and satellite television as an alternative to network programming.

---

[5] Sherri Burr, *Television and Societal Affects*, 4 No. 2 J. GENDER, RACE, & JUST. 160 n. 2 (Spring 2001).

A. THE TELEVISION PROCESS

Similar to the film process, television shows begin with someone pitching an idea to a person with the power to "green-light" the show. While the pitch season has traditionally been in the fall, this is changing as networks begin seeking new material for their schedules throughout the entire year.

Brandon Tartikoff had such green-light power as an executive at NBC. In his book, *The Last Great Ride,* he describes his favorite all time pitch. Legendary actor Marlon Brando walks in his office and describes the show he wants to do based on his life in Tahiti. Brando smiles and says:

> "Well, it's my home movies of Tahiti, of myself in the water, over a number of years, with all these beautiful native women. I've got thousands of minutes of this stuff. And I think I can get the Tahitian government to come in with me on the deal so the price won't be prohibitive. I think it would be a success. You put this thing on in February and it's fifteen below with the windchill factor, how can the guy in Pittsburgh *not* watch naked Tahitian women in the water and Marlon Brando when it comes on at ten p.m.?"[6]

---

[6] Brandon Tartikoff, The Last Great Ride 21-22 (1992).

Brando was unable to obtain the proper permissions from the Tahitian government and his idea never made it on the air, but it did illustrate a quality that Tartikoff values in pitching ideas—enthusiasm. *Id.* at 24. Tartokoff believes there has to be passion at the beginning to sustain five years "when the show is a hundred episodes old and staggering." *Id.* The other qualities that Tartikoff looked for were a connection to real life, story telling ability, and the actor's roles. *Id.* at 25.

Pitches for shows can be very simple, such as "find an ordinary construction worker to masquerade as a millionaire, surround him with beautiful women who didn't know the secret, observe whether they fall in love with him for his imagined millions or his true self." This simple idea, which possessed a connection to real life, was effectively told, and well cast with ordinary individuals, became *Joe Millionaire*, which drew in 40 million viewers for its final episode in February 17, 2003. High ratings and low cost have made shows like *Joe Millionaire* popular with studio executives. However, William Goldman's gripe about the film process, "Nobody knows anything," also applies to television. When the Fox network followed up with *The Next Joe Millionaire* set in Europe, it slumped in the ratings game.

At any given time, four major television networks –ABC, CBS, FOX, and NBC-- may have a program schedule comprised of dramas, game shows, news, reality TV shows, situation comedies, sports, talk shows, and westerns. Some cable channels focus all their programming on one type of show, such as the Comedy Channel, or ESPN, ESPN2, and ESPN news, which concentrate on sports. Cable networks may seek to appeal to a particular gender, such as Life Time, whose slogan is "television for women," or a particular race, such as BET, Black Entertainment Television.

The popularity of show genres varies throughout the years. Westerns were once ubiquitous on network schedules. In the late 1950s there were 30 different westerns on three network channels.[7] *Gunsmoke*, which premiered in 1955 and ran until 1975, became the most popular of the genre and still holds the record as the longest running television show with 633 episodes produced. *Gunsmoke* was set in a raw frontier town in Kansas and featured the 6-foot-7 James Arness as Matt Dillon, the lawman who, as Emily Nusbaum describes, pulled "his pistol one second slower than his opponent, but with better aim." Nusbaum, *supra* note 7. The western then declined in popularity and only recently resurfaced after a long absence on television when HBO launched *Deadwood* in March 2004.[8]

---

[7] *See* Emily Nusbaum, *The Lone Gunman: Justice was a One-Man Job on 'Gunsmoke,'* N.Y. TIMES, Mar. 21, 2004.

[8] *See* Ned Martel, *Resurrecting the Western to Save the Crime Drama*, N.Y. TIMES, Mar. 21, 2004.

Reality television shows, like *Joe Millionaire*, are the most recent phenomena to capture and hold the interest of the viewing public. Reality TV resembles nonfiction books and documentaries, all of which are based on truth. Americans tune in to watch shows like *Survivor*, *The Bachelor*, and *The Apprentice* to observe ordinary participants compete for love and money, and sometimes both. Indeed, one reality show called *For Love or Money* aired during the summers of 2003 and 2004. It required contestants to choose between their love interest and checks worth up to $2 million.

The Apprentice, starring real estate developer Donald Trump, became the first reality show to be featured within a network's signature nightly lineup. *The Apprentice* premiered on a Thursday in January 2004, crouched between *Friends* and *ER* on NBC. It immediately received good reviews and excellent ratings. Its 16 contestants vied to receive a $250,000 job running one of Trump's companies. On its final run, on Thursday, April 15, *The Apprentice* became the number one show of the week when 28 million viewers tuned in to see who Donald Trump would hire. Not without detractors, Trump's competitors accused him of using the show to advertise his conglomerate.

Audience participation versions of reality TV shows ask the public to call in to vote on who should be eliminated from a musical competition show (*American Idol*) or selected to become the husband of a particular female who comes with a $1 million dowry (*Cupid*). Other programs, such as *Extreme Makeover* and *Queer Eye for the Straight Guy*, alter the appearance and/or the living quarters of volunteers. The shows also present the reaction of their family and friends to the vast changes to the person.

Traditionally, networks would order a pilot episode to test the concept. With reality TV, they must order the complete series because the execution of the full work is key. Reality TV shows are shot in their entirety before they are edited and massaged into a story line. Thus, network executives who were comfortable ordering a pilot episode of a new comedy or game show now find themselves ordering the entire four to fifteen episodes of a reality TV show from a pitched idea. For scripted shows, executives who like a comedy or dramatic pilot may purchase three, six, or 13 episodes as a mid-season replacement or the current full season order of 22 episodes.

One major difference between fictional or scripted shows is the former can be syndicated once 100 episodes have been produced. Syndication permits the network and production company to sell all the show's episodes in bulk, and generate tremendous revenue. For example, the Desilu Company realized $60 million between 1955 and 1965 from licensing its television film library, which included *I Love Lucy* and *The Lucy-Desi Show*.

Desilu Productions, Inc. v. C.I.R., 1965 WL 1076 1965 WL 1076 (U.S. Tax Ct. 1965).

I Love Lucy featured a Cuban bandleader and his wacky redheaded wife who was dying to get into show business. Because CBS did not believe that *I Love Lucy* had much chance of success, it gave the Desilu Company the copyrights. Since Desi Arnaz insisted on taping the show instead of broadcasting live, as was customary in the 1950s, he created an extensive film library. Due to syndication, *I Love Lucy* has never been off the air. On any given day, one of its 179 episodes can be seen on a television screen somewhere in the world.

I Love Lucy exemplifies the potential long-run revenue potential generated from syndicated shows. While there has yet to be a syndicated Reality TV show, network executives are attracted to these shows for the enormous initial potential profits generated from not having to pay professional actors or staff union negotiated wages. Indeed, some reality TV stars have been asked to forego joining a union until after they have appeared on the show.

Other reality TV stars have received some form of payment, either as an appearance fee to compensate for their loss of time at their jobs, but more likely because they won the prize money. Trista Rehn received only $10,000 for appearing on both the inaugural *Bachelor* and *Bachelorette*, but then she and Ryan Sutter were paid $1 million to wed on television.

Donald Trump collected $100,000 per episode for his Spring 2004 appearance on *The Apprentice*. Without revealing details, he indicated that he would earn "a lot more" for the fall 2004 follow-up show. Keith Naughton and Mark Peyser, *The World According to Trump*, NEWSWEEK MAG., Mar. 1, 2004.

The doctors, lawyers, accountants, teachers, and airline pilots who win placement on reality TV shows must take several weeks off from their day jobs to film or appear live on a reality TV show. Because *Survivor* requires 39 days of filming, casting director Lynne Spillman says that one third of its participants quit their jobs to participate. Spillman told Newsweek, "The people who apply are at a crossroads." *The lure of shows like Apprentice is a headache for bosses*, NEWSWEEK MAG., Mar. 1, 2004.

Newsweek Magazine also reported that investment banker Kwame Jackson quit Goldman Sachs to appear on *The Apprentice*, attorney Alex Michel resigned from Boston Consulting Group to star in the initial *Bachelor*, and educator Randi Coy was forced to leave her teaching job after taking too much time off to star *in My Big Fat Obnoxious Fiancé*. Michel said, "Anyone who'd take a two-month leave is putting their career progress at risk." *Id*.

Further, reality shows often mandate that participants sign agreements releasing producers from liabilities. The reality show *Survivor* required participants to sign a

"Confidentiality and Life Story Rights Agreement" in which they gave up their right (1) to disclose any trade secrets obtained or learned as a result of participating in the series; (2) to disclose any information about the series prior to broadcast; and (3) agreed that the producer could seek injunctive relief, return of the prize, and recovery of attorneys' fees if the agreement is breached. *See* Seg, Inc. v. Stillman, 2003 WL 21197133 (Cal. Ct. App. 2003).

Other types of shows have different legal issues that arise. Game shows, for example, limit the number of appearances contestants can make on other shows. In *Winston v. NBC*, the California Court of Appeals upheld NBC's right to disqualify a contestant who was not forthcoming about the number of other game shows that he appeared on and to force a forfeiture of the cash he won as a contestant on "Sale of the Century." Winston v. NBC, 231 Cal. App. 3d 540, 282 Cal Rptr. 498 (Cal. App. Ct. 1991). Robert Gelbman sued ABC, claiming that a question on *Who Wants to be a Millionaire* was ambiguous, and thus he was entitled to additional funds because the show provided two possible answer choices that were both correct. The court upheld the release agreement that Gelbman signed, which stated that decisions by the producers and ABC were final. *Gelbman v. Valleycrest Productions, Ltd.* 189 Misc.2d 403, 732 N.Y.S.2d 528 (NY Sup. Ct. 2001).

Talk shows also have participants sign release agreements. Many of them pay for transportation and housing costs for their guests, and some of them pay appearance fees. In *Campoverde v. Sony Pictures Entertainment*, 2002 WL 31163804 (S.D. N. Y. 2002), attorney Susan Chana Lask and her client Juan Campoverde sued the producers of *The Ricki Lake Show* after their scheduled visit did not conform to the negotiated terms. Further, the producers insisted that she sign an union agreement prior to her appearance. When they refused, they were held against their will. The court denied the defendant's motion to dismiss Lask and Campoverde's claims for breach of contract, false imprisonment, and assault and battery.

Fictional shows like comedies and dramas are not immune from lawsuits brought by ordinary people. Michael Constanza sued comedian Jerry Seinfeld, claiming that the fictional character of George Constanza was based on him. Michael Constanza alleged that Seinfeld placed him in "a negative, humiliating light," by attributing a "self-centered nature and unreliability" to the character of George Constanza, who is short, fat, and bald like Michael. Constanza v. Seinfeld, 181 Misc. 2d 562, 564, 693 N.Y.S.2d 897 (N.Y. Sup. Ct. 1999) The court dismissed the case as frivolous because New York courts had rejected such claims for decades and awarded sanctions of $2,500 each against the plaintiff and his attorney. *Id.* at 567.

Network news is competitive in local arenas because it is one of the few shows produced by the affiliate station, which obtains the bulk of its program from the national conglomerate. In its search for ratings, network news shows must also honor people's privacy and are required to follow the legal rules governing other places of employment.

In *Miller v. NBC*, Brownie Miller successfully sued NBC after its television camera crew followed the Los Angeles Fire Department paramedics into her home and filmed the futile attempt to rescue her husband Dave. NBC did not obtain a release agreement and Brownie Miller saw the footage of her husband weeks after his death while flipping channels. The court held that she had a cause of action for trespass, invasion of privacy and intentional infliction of emotional distress. Miller v. NBC, 187 Cal. App. 3d 1463, 232 Cal. Rptr. 668 (Cal. App. Ct. 1986).

In addition to trying to attract audiences with sensational programming, network news shows have tried to capture audiences by choosing attractive anchors. Nevertheless, they must be careful not to commit employment discrimination based on age.

David Minshall successfully sued the McGraw-Hill Broadcasting Company, which does business as KMGH in Denver, Colorado, for age discrimination after it decided not to renew his contract when he was over the age of

50. Minshall v. McGraw Hill Broadcasting Co., 323 F.3d 1273 (10th Cir. 2003). When news director Melissa Klinzing decided to reach a younger demographic, she moved individuals over 40 years of age to the ten o'clock nightly news and increasingly gave other individuals over 40 less favorable job assignments. Eventually KMGH instructed Klinzing not to renew anyone's contract over the age of 40. The court found that Klinging and KMGH had engaged in age discrimination. Klinzing had urged Minshall to adopt "a more youthful presentation." She also said one person was "too fucking old" for the news format, and said "old people should die" in reference to her own father. *Id.* at 1281.

In 2001, a group of 50 television writers sued 51 studios, network television companies, and talent agencies for age discrimination, claiming that they had been gray-listed. James Langton, *'Greylisted" Hollywood Writers to Sue for Age Discrimination*, SUNDAY TELEGRAPH, Aug. 5, 2001. The class action lawsuit alleged a "systematic and pervasive pattern of age discrimination" against writers over 40 and sought damages of $200 million. *Id.*

After the initial class action was dismissed, 150 television writers filed 23 separate class action lawsuits in Los Angeles Superior Court in 2002. The lawsuit claimed that in 1997-98 season, two-thirds of the prime-time series did not employ a single writer over the age of 50. The writers cited remarks from Marta

Kauffmann, the co-creator of NBC's Friends, who said, "Once you hit 40, you can't do it anymore." Gary David Goldberg, the producer of ABC's *Spin City*, was quoted as saying his program had "no writers on the set over the age of 29—by design." www.writerscase.com.

In February 2003, Judge McCoy dismissed all of the twenty-three separate class actions pending in Los Angeles Superior Court. Plaintiffs then appealed that decision with respect to the talent agency defendant cases. The California Court of Appeal granted agreed to consolidate all appeals for the purpose of reviewing Judge McCoy's decision concerning all defendants. A hearing in the matter took place June 29, 2004, with a ruling expected later in 2004. *Id.*

Discrimination issues merit due consideration in Hollywood.

B. TELEVISION DIVERSITY

Television also impacts how viewers in a diverse society perceive ethnic groups other than themselves. It was several years after the first TV set was invented in the 1920s before African-Americans and some other ethnic groups began to make appearances on television. In 1939, Clarence Muse became the first African-American to appear on television when he was featured on Los Angeles station W6XAO. Bob Howard was the first African-American to have his own network program, which ran between 1948 and 1949. Burr, *supra* note 5, at 160-161. During the 1950s through the 1990s, more Americans of diverse backgrounds made appearances in a variety of network shows, from musical variety, to dramas and comedies. With the opening up of television to more groups came criticism that the programming was stereotypical, and thus reinforced negative group images.

Several efforts were made to diversify television programming and images by encouraging the hiring of more producers, actors, and crews from a variety of racial and ethnic backgrounds. In the 1970s and 1980s, the Federal Communications Commission adopted programs to encourage minority ownership of television stations as connected to increasing the number of minorities who appear in front of and behind the camera.

A few Caucasians challenged these programs as violating the equal protection component of the Fifth Amendment in *Metro Broadcasting v. FCC*, 497 U.S. 547 (1990). The Supreme Court upheld the programs, finding that the interest in enhancing broadcast diversity is "an important governmental objective and is therefore a sufficient basis for the Commission's minority ownership policies." *Id.* at 567-568. The Court noted that these minority ownership policies were "appropriately limited in extent and duration, and subject to reassessment and reevaluation by the Congress prior to any extension or reenactment." *Id.* at

594. The Supreme Court overruled this decision five years later in *Adarand Constructors v. Pena*, 515 U.S. 200 (1995).

Four years later, the major networks announced that their lineups for their fall 1999 season would consist of twenty-six new shows, not one of which featured a lead character who was African American, Asian American, Native American, or Latino.[9] After a threatened boycott and numerous meetings between Hollywood executives and the NAACP, the networks made adjustments to their schedules and added more minority characters to their planned shows and augmented the number shows that featured minority story lines.

In March 2004, ABC and Touchstone TV announced a pact with the Directors Guild of America to place women and minority directors behind the camera on at least 20 television episodes during the 2004-2005 season. Michael Schneider, *Diversity Directive: Touchstone, ABC, DGA tout hiring effort*, VARIETY, Mar. 30, 2004. The plan assigns a diverse group of at least 10 directors to 10 half-hour comedy episodes and 10 hour-long drama segments of new and returning series. *Id.*

---

[9] Gary Williams, *Don't Try to Adjust Your Television— I'm Black": Ruminations on the Recurrent Controversy over the Whiteness of TV*, 4 No. 2 J. GENDER RACE & JUST. 99 (Spring 2001).

Native Americans have faced different issues than African Americans on television. Because of the early popularity of westerns, they were regularly featured on television as well as in films. Chris Eyre, the first Native American director to produce a nationally released film, bemoans "the lack of representation of Indian people in the mainstream media." He thinks that a "politically correct romanticism of what Indians should be" gets depicted, but not "the average Joes of Indian country who are not romantic." Burr and Henslee, *supra* note 1, at 563. Eyre once told The New York Times "the only thing that has been more detrimental to Indians than religion has been John Ford movies" because he believes John Ford focused on the period of Indian wars and never investigated the culture that grew out of that period. *Id.* Eyre says that he is less interested in portraying positive images, than he is in "depicting accurate images." *Id.*

The impact of stereotypical images has been assessed in studies. A 1998 study conducted on behalf of Children Now, a nonprofit children's advocacy group, revealed that children "more often associate positive qualities such as financial and academic success, leadership, and intelligence with White characters, and negative qualities such as law breaking, financial hardship, laziness, and goofy behavior with minority characters." Burr, *supra* note 3, at 180. Fifty-eight percent of the children said they see Caucasians on television as having a lot of money, but only eight percent perceived minority characters as having a lot of money. *Id.* Conversely, forty-seven reported seeing minority characters break the law but only six percent reported seeing Caucasians break the law. *Id.* The children also observed how often they saw their own race depicted: 71% of Caucasian children saw their race portrayed very often compared with only 42% of African-Americans and 22% of Hispanic-Americans. *Id.*

Hae-Kyong Bang and Bonnie B. Reece analyzed the content of 813 commercials in children's television programs and found that minorities were "more likely than Caucasians to have minor roles and to be portrayed in certain product categories, settings, and relationships." Burr and Henslee, *supra* note 1, at 565. Bang and Reece found that Blacks and Asian Americans were over-represented and Hispanics were somewhat underrepresented in commercials, but that they were less likely to appear in major roles, and less likely to appear as a group compared to whites. *Id.* at 568. Bang and Reece postulated that these portrayals could potentially harm children's self-perception and recommended that conscious efforts "be made to portray all ethnic groups fairly and in a non-stereotypical manner so that minority groups are seen as valued consumers well integrated into the society." *Id.* at 571-572.

C. TELEVISION AND SOCIETY

Given the pervasive nature of television, it is not surprising that it has had and continues to have a profound impact on society. In the United States, television reaches a broad array of ethnic groups and homes.

Television programming can be educational, teaching its young viewers how to read and adults how to cook. Because several shows focus on the law, some Americans learn about their legal rights from watching television. Nevertheless, some people have claimed that television has had a negative impact on their lives, making them fat, lethargic, and sometimes pathological.

One study tested the impact of television viewing on children's behavior. The study divided school children participants into three groups: "group 1 watched television for two hours or less per day; group 2, for two to for hours per day; and group 3, for more than four hours per day." Karl E. Miller, *Children's Behavior Correlates with Television Viewing*, 67, No.3 AMER. FAM. PHYSICIAN 593-4 (Feb. 1, 2003). The study determined that "[o]verall viewing time had a negative relationship with social and school achievement scores." *Id.* The study further found that increased viewing time correlated with "social problems, thought problems, attention problems, delinquent behavior, aggressive behavior, and externalization." *Id.* The study recommended that "parents limit their children's television viewing time to two hours or less per day."

Another study determined people could become addicted to television. The indicators of dependence on television were (1) television consumed large amounts of their time; (2) they watched TV longer or more often than they intended; (3) they made repeated unsuccessful efforts to cut down their TV watching: (4) they withdrew from or gave up important social, family, or occupational activities in order to watch television; and (5) they reported "withdrawal" like symptoms of subjective discomfort when deprived of TV. Robert D. McIlwraith, *"I'm Addicted to Television": The Personality, Imagination, and TV Watching Patterns of Self-identified TV addicts.* 42 N.3 J. BROADCAST. & ELECT. MEDIA, at 371 (Summer 1998). The study's authors postulated that television addiction had "similarities to pathological gambling." *Id.*

In a study reported on in *Scientific American,* Robert Kubey and Mihaly Csikszentimahalyi revealed that people tend to turn on the television out of boredom, and yet their study using electroencephalograph (or EEG) found that people watching television "showed less mental stimulation, as measured by alpha brain-wave production, during viewing than during reading." Robert Kubey & Mihaly Csikszentmihalyi, *Television Addiction Is No Mere Metaphor,* SCIENTIFIC AMERICAN (February 2002). Further, they discovered that the sense of relaxation "ends when the set is turned off, but the feelings of passivity and lowered alertness continued." *Id.*

The parents of Ronny Zamora sued NBC, CBS, and ABC, after their son killed their 83-year-old neighbor Elinor Haggart. The parents charged that Ronny had become involuntary addicted to and subliminally intoxicated by the excessive violence on television from the age of five until 15 when he shot Haggart. The parents contended that Ronny was stimulated and incited to duplicate the atrocities he saw on television.

The district court, however, dismissed *Zamora v. CBS* for failure to state a claim. 480 F.Supp. 199 (S.D. Fla. 1979). The court expressed concerned that the complaint did not cite a particular program or distinguish among the networks in his viewing pattern. The court was reluctant to expand Florida tort law to create a duty on the part of the networks to anticipate a minor's voracious, yet voluntary, intake of violence, his parents acquiescence, and that the minor would respond with a criminal act. *Id.* at 202-203.

This court sent a message that urges parents to take responsibility to limit the television viewing of their children, particularly if it is having a negative impact on their development.

D. CABLE & SATELLITE TELEVISON

The increasing availability of cable and satellite television to more households will only augment the opportunities of most Americans to watch television. An appliance owner who had difficulty selling television sets in rural areas because of poor reception invented cable television, originally christened Community Antenna Television or CATV. To solve this problem of limited signals, John Watson put up an antenna on top of a large utility pole and installed it on top of a nearby Pennsylvania mountain. As television signals were received and transported to his store, Watson sold more sets. *See* http://www.telecom.ksu.edu/cable/history.html.

Cable television has since grown into a successful fee-paid business with 60 million subscribers. By 1992, cable served 60% of American households and was projected to grow beyond 70%. *See* Turner v. FCC, 520 U.S. 180, 197 (1997). Digital and satellite transmission became more popular in the 1990s as it offered even more channels and promised an even clearer picture by up-linking signals to satellites orbiting in space and beaming those signals to dishes. *See* Satellite Broadcasting & Communications Ass'n v. F.C.C. 275 F.3d 337, 344 (4th Cir. 2001).

By the year 2001, only 20% of American households relied exclusively on the major broadcast networks for their television programming. *Id.* Cable and satellite companies served around 80% of the television households, with cable accounting for 67% and satellite carriers responsible for 13%. *Id.* While broadcast networks rely on advertising as their primary source of revenues, cable and satellite companies depend on subscription fees. One difference between cable and satellite TV is that cable uses local wire networks to deliver their signals, whereas satellite TV is a national service that transmits a single beam covering the entire continental U.S. and can deliver between 450 and 500 channels. *Id.* at 345.

The Federal Communications Commission regulates all television, including network, cable, and satellite transmissions. In the 1960s, it expressly preempted any state and local regulation of cable television. Capital Cities Cable, Inc. v. Crisp, 467 U.S. 691 (1984). In 1965, the FCC promulgated rules requiring cable systems to carry the signals of all local stations in their areas. Oklahoma, which had deemed it unlawful to sell and consume alcoholic beverages within the state, passed legislation requiring these same cable television operators to delete all advertising for alcoholic beverages contained in the out-of-state signals that retransmit into Oklahoma. The Supreme Court concluded that since the FCC preempted cable regulation, Oklahoma lacked the power to regulate cable broadcasters. *Id.*

Cable companies have also challenged Congressional mandates regulating cable television, particularly the "must carry" provisions that require them to offer local programming. In *Turner v. FCC*, the Supreme Court found "a substantial basis to support Congress's conclusion that a real threat justified enactment of the must-carry provisions." 520 U.S. at 196. The threat that concerned Congress was that cable companies possessed a local monopoly over cable households, with only one percent of communities being served by more than one cable system. As such, the Court noted they could "silence the voice of competing speakers with a mere flick of the switch." *Id.* at 197 (quoting Turner v. FCC, 512 U.S. 622, 656).

Before passing the Cable Television Consumer Protection and Consumer Act of 1992, Congress reviewed evidence that because of the competition between network and cable television for the same advertisers, cable television has substantial incentives to drop broadcast stations. One cable-industry executive said, "[O]ur job is to promote cable television, not broadcast television." *Id.* at 201. The Supreme Court observed, "By the time the Cable Act was passed, 1,261 broadcast stations had been dropped for at least one year, in a total of 7,945 incidents." *Id.* at 205. The Court concluded that "must carry" serves the Government's interest by ensuring "that a number of local broadcasters retain cable carriage, with the concomitant audience access and advertising revenues needed to support a multiplicity of stations." *Id.* at 213.

When direct broadcast satellite service became a major force in the market for delivering television service, they also resisted carrying broadcast networks. To counter this resistance, Congress passed the Satellite Home

Viewer Improvement Act (SHVIA) in 1999 to require satellite carriers to provide secondary transmissions to subscribers of all local channels. The SHVIA Act included a "carry one, carry all rule," mandating satellite carriers who chose to carry one broadcast station in a local market "to carry all requesting stations within that market." Satellite Broadcasting & Communications Ass'n, 275 F.3d at 342. To provide an incentive to satellite carriers, Congress created a statutory copyright license that allows them to carry the signals of local broadcast television stations without obtaining authorization from the holders of copyrights in the individual programs aired by the stations. *Id.*

When the "carry one, carry all" rule was challenged by satellite carriers, the court of appeals held that the rule does not violate the Constitution. It observed that the rule was a "narrowly tailored means of promoting the government's important ends of preserving a vibrant mix of local broadcast outlets for over-the-air viewers and minimizing the unintended side affects of SHVIA's statutory copyright license on local broadcast advertising markets." *Id.* at 365. As such, the court concluded, "The carry one, carry all rule is therefore consistent with the First Amendment." *Id.*

Most recently, the FCC created controversy with its proposal to relax the federal rules on media ownership that restrict conglomerates from owning more than one television station in the same city, or both a newspaper and TV or radio station in the same city. In *Prometheus Radio Project v. F.C.C.*, 2004 WL 1405975 (3rd Cir. 2004), the court of appeals blocked the new rules, which lifted a 1975 ban on such consolidation of ownership, from taking affect. The court remanded the FCC's order for additional justification on its chosen numerical limits for local television ownership, local radio ownership and cross-ownership of medial within local markets. *Id.*

The new rules turned out to be controversial in unexpected circles. Ted Turner, who built CNN into a major player and then sold it to Time Warner, opposed the rules. In an op-ed piece, he postulated that the proposed change would "stifle debate, inhibit new ideas and shut out smaller business trying to compete. If these rules had been in place in 1970, it would have been virtually impossible for me to start Turner Broadcasting or, 10 years later, to launch CNN." Ted Turner, *Monopoly or Democracy*, WASHINGTON POST, May 30, 2003.

In another op-ed piece, Bob Hebert argued that the FCC had become cozy with the very telecommunications and broadcasting industries they regulate. Hebert cited a Center for Public Integrity study that examined the travel records of FCC employees and found that "over the last eight years, commissioners and staff members have taken 2,500 trips costing $42.8 million that were 'primarily' paid for by members of the telecommunications and broadcast industries." Bob Hebert, *Cozy with the F.C.C.*, N.Y. TIMES, June 5, 2003, at A35. The top destination for these FCC trips was Las Vegas (330 trips), followed by New Orleans (173 trips) and New York (102). International destinations included London, Buenos Aires, and Beijing.

The consequences of FCC plans to deregulate the industry can already be seen in the decline of independently produced television shows. According to another study, for the fall 2003 prime time schedule, the four networks had a stake in 67% of the programs they aired, compared to 32% in the fall of 1992. Only 2% of the fall 2003 lineup came from independent producers compared with 30% in 1992. *See* Bill Carter and Jim Rutenberg, *Deregulating the Media*, N.Y. TIMES, June 3, 2003, at C1.

CHAPTER 3

THE MUSIC INDUSTRY

The music business encompasses a lucrative component of the entertainment industry. During the first half of 2004, the music industry sold 305.72 million units.[10] Pricewaterhouse Coopers projects that by 2008, U.S. spending on music will grow to $13.98 billion, a $2 billion jump from the 2003 spending level. Compact discs (CDs) represent 98% of the sales, with cassettes, LPs and DVDs accounting for the remainder. *Id.*

Music's popularity stems from its intimate connection to and reflection of society. Groups produce different types of sounds to reflect their immediate cultural experiences. Music that is popular with one generation easily becomes passé or old school with the next. Classical music is an art form that originated in Europe with great composers ranging from Mozart and Haydn to Beethoven and Ravel contributing to its popularity. While classical music is still

---

[10] Phil Gallo, *Music Sales sing in first half,* VARIETY MAG. June 30, 2004, *available at* http://www.variety. com/index.asp?layout=print_story&articleid=VR1179 07248&categoryid=16.

played by symphony orchestras around the world, it struggles to modernize and become relevant to a current age when youth prefer heavy metal bands like Metalica and the Flashing Pumpkins or rap artists like Dr. Dre and Ice T.

African-Americans created spiritual music during their enslavement. Songs such as "Go Down Moses" and "Swing Lo, Sweet Chariot" reflected their loss of freedom and hopes for better lives. The blues evolved during the Jim Crow decades that followed emancipation as Blacks were physically free but had yet to achieve political and economic liberation.

Rock and roll became a popular upbeat music form during the 1950s and 1960s, accompanied by and derived from rhythm and blues and soul music. In the 1990s and the decade of 2000, hip hop and rap music became the battle cry for a generation that felt trapped in urban areas, held back from the American dream, and at war with the police. While all music written for voice can be termed poetry set to instrumental music, rap music takes this to the extreme as the words are spoken in a beat to limited accompaniment.

Music regularly crosses ethnic and racial boundaries, leading to a shaping and sharing of cultural values. Like Picasso who was inspired by visits to Africa to create his impressionist work, Elvis Presley frequented blues and jazz bars in Memphis prior to fashioning his unique form of rock and roll. Contralto Marian Anderson was the first Black to sing at the Metropolitan Opera House in New York City, making her debut in 1955 as Ulrica in Verdi's *Un Ballo in Maschera* (A Masked Ball). In 2004, white musician Eminem won the Grammy Award for Best Male Rap Solo Performance.

This chapter begins by discussing the music process and the major players in the business. For centuries, musicians have made money from three primary sources: publishing, performing, and touring. A secondary source for some, although primary to others, is teaching. This chapter discusses the three primary sources, as well as indebtedness, a legal issue confronting musicians at a higher rate than other entertainers. As a consequence, musicians often become ensnared in bankruptcy and tax pitfalls that jeopardize their financial well-being.

A. THE MUSIC PROCESS

As music has evolved over the centuries, so have the methods of capturing it for posterity. Mozart and his cohorts published sheet music and performed it before royalty and nobility in private musicales and elaborate concert halls. Composers like Elton John continue to produce sheet music available for purchase at music stores. Modern musicians are, nevertheless, more likely to perform at public venues for several hundred or several thousand music-loving souls. Superstar musicians may play in stadiums containing 100,000 seats.

Contemporary musicians also have an advantage over creators of the 1600s and 1700s in that they can record their songs in a studio on machines and later release them for public consumption. In the month or so before he was killed, Tupac Shakur practically lived in a studio with his group, creating numerous songs that have been released as CDs after his untimely demise. The mechanical recording of music provides another means of achieving immortality for creators whose works resonate with the public.

Interviews with musicians and bands of various genres reveal there is no one true path to becoming a successful musician. One truism often repeated in the music business is that an artist gets his whole life to produce his first CD and only six months to produce the next one if the first is a hit.

Keali'i Reichel,[11] a professor of Hawaiian language and culture at Maui Community College, often crooned in the shower and around his home until his friends began begging him to record his voice. In 1994, Reichel independently produced and released a collection of Hawaiian traditional and contemporary music called

---

[11] The author's interviews with Mr. Reichel were first broadcast on *Arts Talk* in Honolulu, Hawaii (Olelo Cable Broadcast, April 1999).

Kawaipunahele to considerable accolades. His debut album received five 1995 Na Hoku Hanohano Awards, the Hawaiian equivalent of the Grammys. He won Popular Hawaiian Album of the Year; Male Vocalist of the Year; Album of the Year; Entertainer of the Year (by public vote); and Most Promising New Artist. His success meant he had only a few months to produce his next album Lei Hali'a, which also won five Hoku awards. In the decade following his debut album, Reichel played in venues as diverse as the Hollywood Bowl and Carnegie Hall, and opened for LeAnn Rimes, Celine Dion, and Sting.

Bob Guiney[12] started singing soft rock music as part of a group calling itself "Fat Amy" in 1992. At the time, he and his band members were college students at Michigan State University. Fellow band member Matt Jackson says, "We began as a bar band, playing whatever gigs we could get." Early on, Guiney and Jackson served as the band's managers and booking agents. They shopped their demo tapes around town to line up gigs.

"Fat Amy" changed its name to "The Bob Guiney Band" after Guiney was cast on the reality television shows *The Bachelorette* and

---

[12] The author interviewed Mr. Guiney and his band members after they played a set in Ned's in Albuquerque, New Mexico, on February 24, 2004. The complete text of the interview can be found in Burr and Henslee, *supra* note 1, at 322-324.

The Bachelor. When he became the popular "Bachelor Bob," Wind-up Records pursued him and offered his band publishing and recording contracts. Wind-up Records also underwrote a radio tour to get radio stations to play his band's music.

Matt Jackson explains the necessity of bands traveling the country to perform at venues sponsored by radio stations. "It used to be the stations played 60 or 70 records throughout the day," he says. "Now they play 17-19 records all day long. We're trying to get in that mix so that people are hearing our songs and wanting to buy our CDs."

After Wind-up Records decided to promote the Bob Guiney band, they acquired a team consisting of agents, managers and lawyers to assist them. "When you get to this level," says Jackson, "You can no longer do it all."

Other musicians have been discovered singing at karaoke bars, or in their churches. Tina Turner sang gospel music in church choirs before being discovered by Ike Turner. After marrying her, he changed her name from Anna Mae Bullock to her stage moniker.

Since there is no one path into the music business, the challenge for musicians is to produce their best work at all times. They never know who will drop by a bar, watch them perform on a reality TV show, or even listen to them sing in the shower. Once they enter the business, they become one of the players in the industry.

B. THE PLAYERS

The technology revolution enables musicians like Reichel to produce albums at low cost, either by establishing sound booths in their own homes or by renting space at less expensive fees than before. Some of the music industry's major players are (1) composers, performers, producers; (2) music publishers; (3) performance rights societies; (4) recording companies; and (5) tour promoters. This section examines their contributions to the music process.

1. COMPOSERS, PERFORMERS, PRODUCERS

As with films where the blueprint is the script making the writer a key player in movie-making, crafting songs launches the music process. Some composers write both the lyrics and music. Others like Richard Rodgers and Oscar Hammerstein collaborate with one contributing the lyrics and the other producing music. The Rogers and Hammerstein partnership created legendary musicals like *Oklahoma*, *South Pacific*, and *The Sound of Music* that are still performed in the theater today and have been turned into film musicals.

Performers supply their unique voices or skills to the songwriters' material. While Charles

Fox wrote "Killing Me Softly With His Song," Roberta Flack gave it a soulful rendition.

Performers can pick and choose from a wealth of material, some of which is in the public domain, available for anyone to use. For centuries, classical music artists made a living performing the works of composers who left behind an enormous body of work that is now free. More recent creations may be protected by copyright laws, which require performers to pay royalties to the owner(s) of songs. Performers who write their own music have a safer shot at immortality, as others may play their music into eternity.

Once performers decide to record their music in a mechanical form so that it can be sold to the public as a CD, LP, or DVD, they often seek producers to assist them. As in the film industry, producers help bring the final product together. They can find the perfect material for a particular artist's voice and then choose the sound engineer who puts it all into an appropriate form.

Gifted producers often possess exceptional ears and can tell immediately when a note sounds sharp or falls flat. Good producers, as demonstrated in the film *Laurel Canyon*, spend a great deal of time with performers helping them mold the right sounds into an album they can sell.

Producers receive upfront fees and a share of the royalties. Often they are paid before the artist receives his or her share. They often earn more than performers.

2. MUSIC PUBLISHERS

A principle source of income for Mozart was the concerts he gave of his own work. Another source was publishing his music.

Music publishing houses assist artists by reproducing, selling, and licensing their work. Charles Fox's songs, along with those of millions of composers, can be purchased either solo or in a compilation in stores that sell sheet music. The music publishing company authorizes these sales and receives revenue in return, which it shares with the composer.

Publishers also license other uses of their artists' works. Under the copyright laws, which will be discussed in more detail in Chapter 5, any performer can make an exact cut of a song and pay royalties set by statute to the music publisher. The publisher then splits the royalties with the names on the copyright.

If a movie or television producer wants to synchronize a song to a film or show, they must obtain a synchronization license from the music publisher. If the producer is interested in a particular rendition of the song they must also obtain a mechanical license from the recording company. This license is necessary when a film producer wants to incorporate a sound recording into the soundtrack of a taped commercial television production. *See* Agee v. Paramount Communications, 59 F.3d 317 (2nd Cir. 1995).

Further if the recording company grants a right to synchronize a master recording to a film that includes the right to exploit, distribute, market and perform the picture "by any means or methods now or hereafter known," that grant includes distribution on video cassettes. *See* Platinum Record v. Lucasfilm, Ltd., 566 F.Supp. 226 (D.N.J. 1983).

Some of these licenses can be acquired from performance rights societies.

3. PERFORMANCE RIGHTS SOCIETIES

Composers, songwriters, lyricists, and music publishers join performance rights societies like ASCAP (American Society of Composers, Authors, and Publishers) and BMI (Broadcast Music Industry) because they keep track of wide-ranging uses of songs. Membership in performance rights societies is generally open to musicians of all genres of music.

Performance rights societies license and distribute royalties for public performance of copyrighted works. They collect fees from radio stations, broadcast and cable television networks, Internet users, and live and recorded performances. Even when a company plays music on their telephones or in their elevators, they may owe royalties to performance rights societies. These societies redistribute their collections to their members based on statistical sampling of the songs in their catalogue. The higher percentage play of a particular song, the more revenue the owner receives. BMI and ASCAP sell single use, single fee licenses, and blanket licenses. The latter's fees are based on the company's revenue, and give the licensee the right to exploit any song in the catalogue.

Established in 1927, the Harry Fox Agency, based in New York, also issues blanket licenses, although it concentrates on mechanical licenses. Harry Fox licenses the use of copyrighted musical compositions for use on CDs, records, tapes, and certain digital configurations. During the early days of rap music, when sampling other artists' work was common, the musicians were unaware that they needed a mechanical license to make use of another person's song. Harry Fox notes on its website, www.harryfox.com/mechanical, that its mechanical license does not include the right to display or reprint lyrics or the right to print sheet music, nor does it cover the use of songs on karaoke machines. It advises readers to contact the publisher(s) directly for those rights. *Id.*

SESAC, the Society of European Stage Authors & Composers, is a privately held corporation with offices in London, Los Angeles,

Nashville and New York. Initially SESAC's repertory was limited to European and gospel music, but it has diversified to include dance hits, rock classics, Latin music, jazz, country, and contemporary music, according to its website, www.sesac.com.

JASRAC, the Japanese Society for Rights of Authors, Composers and Publishers, was founded in 1939 to assist Japanese musicians and publishers. It initially set fees for concerts, dramatic representation, radio broadcasting, talkies, and publications. JASRAC, THE ORGANIZATION AND OPERATIONS OF JASRAC 4-8 (Oct. 1, 1992). In an interview at their corporate offices in 1993, several JASRAC officers said that they actively pursue Karaoke bars and machines to sell them licenses.

There are a host of performance rights societies throughout the world. Countries that have a music industry often have a performance rights society to monitor the uses of the music.

4. RECORDING COMPANIES

The music industry contains companies that record and distribute songs for musicians. Musicians seek record contracts but they often find that recording companies will not risk enormous sums to advance their careers until they see the band perform. Yet, it may be difficult to obtain engagements until they have a CD that demonstrates their abilities. Many bands resolve this catch-22 by spending their own resources to record an initial demo tape.

Because of the enormous risk associated with bringing out new artists, recording companies try to lower their exposure by sending out scouts, called A & R (artist and repertoire) people to clubs to find the fresh, new talent. Recording companies are then known to sign artists to draconian contracts and advance them money against their future revenue stream. This places many artists in financial holes from which they never resurface.

Attorney Peter Thall says that many of his clients believe that the more money they owe their recording company, the more likely the company is to promote them. Thall finds the contrary to be true. He says, companies prefer "to write off the expense as a bad debt than to throw good money after bad."[13]

Mariah Carey's situation proves Thall's point. In January 2002, Virgin Records terminated its contract with Carey after her "Glitter" album sold only 500,000 copies in the United States. Virgin Records paid Carey $28 million to cancel their agreement, and allowed her to retain the $21 million she received when initially signing with them. The company essentially paid Carey $98 for every album it sold, this after having cut the cost of the single

---

[13] PETER M. THALL, WHAT THEY'LL NEVER TELL YOU ABOUT THE MUSIC BUSINESS 28 (2002).

"Loverboy" to 49 cents to help it climb the charts. Virgin Records' risk, valued at $80 million for four albums, was based on Carey having sold more than 150 million singles and albums worldwide since her debut in 1990. However, Carey developed personal problems and was hospitalized during summer of 2001 just prior to the release of the "Glitter" album and film. Virgin Records decided to write-off the deal after one album and not take further chances with the remaining ones.

Carey's situation also illustrates why record companies will fight to protect their interest if an artists produces a hit while under contract. In *Isley v. Motown Record Corp.*, the recording company sought a declaration that the Isley Brothers were under contract when they recorded "It's Your Thing," which sold 1,750,000 copies. 69 F.R.D. 12 (S.D.N.Y. 1975). At issue was whether the Isley Brothers recorded "It's Your Thing" in November 1968 while under contract with Motown or in January 1969 after they had been released from their agreement. Their deal required Motown to advance money for recording sessions and in return Motown would own all copyrights to the Isley's compositions and all master recordings.

A jury determined the song had been recorded after January 1969 and belonged exclusively to the Isley Brothers. The district judge, however, set aside the jury's verdict, finding it based on contradictory and self-serving testimony from the Isley Brothers. At trial, the Isleys repudiated their own earlier sworn testimony by characterizing it variously as a lie and false. The judge found their first testimony supported the contrary conclusion that they created the music in November 1968.

In their 1969-70 depositions, the Isley brothers testified that after finding the back-up band, they asked Motown to advance them money for a recording session in which they planned to record music of their own. The tape of the November 6, 1968 session disappeared. At trial, the Isley brothers said they asked Motown for the recording session money because they were broke and needed to buy Christmas presents and pay household expenses. They later said their mother threw out the tape of the November 6, 1968, session.

The court queried whether the mother of successful recording artists would throw out any tape, let alone one a month old? The court also questioned why had the Isleys not sent the tape immediately to Motown as they had agreed to do in their November 1 letter requesting the funds? Based upon Motown's proof of contemporaneous writings and the testimony of musicians who played at the November 6 session, the court concluded that the Isely Brothers' trial testimony constituted false evidence. After determining that the jury's verdict resulted "in a miscarriage of justice" based on untrue statements, the court ordered a new trial.

Many musicians feel that recording companies do not offer fair deals. However, courts rarely set aside contracts as unconscionable on that basis alone. While musicians in the early stages of their careers may have limited negotiating power, they should have attorneys explain their contracts so they at least understand the bargain they are making and do not overspend while expecting to receive royalties that never materialize.

The assignment clause in contracts, for example, can lead to bands ending with a different recording company if a merger takes place. With the consolidation of entertainment industry, executives who nurtured a particular band's career may depart, abandoning them to the mercy of new personnel who have less of a vested interest in their success and want to develop their own discoveries.

California law considers recording agreements as contracts for personal services. California Civil Code § 3423 mandates that these agreements guarantee the artists will make a minimum of $9,000 the first year of the contract, $12,000 the second year, and $15,000 in years three through seven. Cal. Civ. Code § 3423 (A)(i). Further, section 2855 of the California Labor Code limits the enforcement of personal service contracts to seven years. Cal. Lab. Code § 2855(a).

5. TOUR PROMOTERS

For centuries, musicians have supported themselves, at least in part, through touring. In the late 1700s, Mozart toured often as a child; at one point he was on the road in Europe for two years with his father. He performed his own concertos in concert halls and in the salons of wealthy and royal Europeans. This touring provided reliable sources of income, along with teaching, an activity that he never liked.[14]

Bands tour for the same reasons that authors conduct book signings. By placing their names in the public eye, they spawn more interest in their creative products. Musicians expand their fan base through touring. Musicians also generate additional sales for their records and concert related material.

Nevertheless, tours can be expensive and bands have to be careful not to spend more on the tour than they generate in revenue. Unbeknownst to some bands, when recording companies advance revenue to support the transportation, living, and other expenses associated with a tour, they recoup those costs from the band's royalties.

Bands sign agreements with tour promoters and/or their companies. Tour promoters contract to bring bands to particular locales and make all the local arrangements. The promoters

---

[14] *See* PETER GAY, MOZART (Books on Tape 2000).

expect bands to perform in a professional manner and give a great concert.

Tom Moffatt[15] began bringing musicians to Hawaii in the 1950s. He worked with Colonel Parker to set up Elvis Presley concerts in 1957, and again in 1960 right after Presley got out of the army and 1973 while he was in the islands to film *Blue Hawaii.* Over the decades, Moffatt has dealt with a range of issues in staging an elaborate concert. He says the biggest show and the most unusual was when Michael Jackson hired two Russian cargo planes to fly in an army tank that was part of his act. This did not surprise Moffatt because he knows of pianists who ship their own Yamaha piano to Japan. He says musicians become attached to and prefer using particular instruments.

Depending on the size of the show, Moffatt may have to hire local technicians to help with the set-up, although each band usually brings in a specialist to supervise the work. The size of the show's equipment and the accompanying entourage affect the cost of the show and the associated ticket prices.

When setting up a concert, promoters enter into agreements laying out the parameters of the tours. These negotiations may take place in

---

[15] The author interviewed Tom Moffatt in Honolulu, Hawaii, just days before Janet Jackson came to Honolulu to perform. The interview ran on *Arts Talk* (Olelo Cable Broadcast, February 16, 1999).

person, on the phone, by fax, through e-mail, or any other available means of communication. Moffatt says that after he realized the 1997 Michael Jackson show would sell out in a few hours, he called Jackson's people to ask if he could add another show to accompany the Friday one. Jackson's agents agreed, but wouldn't confirm a date as they couldn't say if it would be on a Saturday or Sunday as Jackson normally did not do two shows in a row. Moffatt then announced a second engagement without a firm date. He simply had the tickets stamped TBA. Both shows sold out in one day.

Because of their sometimes frantic and unpredictable nature, setting up a tour can lead to misunderstandings if the two parties aren't determined to make the event happen. In April 1996, pop singer Michael Bolton and Australian corporation Michael Coppel Promotions (MCP) exchanged telefaxes and telephone calls to set up an eight-concert Australian tour between May 14 to 28, 1996. In return for performing in various Australian cities, Bolton was to be paid "the greater of $1,200,000 or 85% of the net door receipts of ticket sales." Michael Coppel Promotions v. Bolton, 982 F. Supp. 950, 952 (S.D.N.Y. 1997). With the consent of Bolton's booking agent, MCP commenced ticket sales for six of the eight tour dates.

After problems developed with the Korean leg of Bolton's tour, his representative canceled the Australian tour, citing problems with ticket sales. MCP sued Bolton, who insisted that no oral or written agreement had been reached because many items remained to be worked out. There was conflict over the entourage's accommodations. For Bolton's previous Australian tour, MCP furnished lodging only for 29 people. For the 1996 tour, Bolton requested that MCP provide breakfast and hotel rooms for 42.

The district court found that although some details remained to be ironed out, the parties had indeed manifested intent to enter into a contract. The court noted that MCP had partially performed the contract based on the oral agreement by selling tickets. The court concluded that a contract has been formed if an initial meeting of the minds has occurred to the contract's material terms. *Id.* at 954.

The *Bolton* case illustrates that once an agreement has been reached and the other party proceeds to act on it, the performer is expected to show up. European concert promoter Marcel Abram sued Michael Jackson for canceling two New Year's Eve 1999 concerts. To celebrate the millennium, Jackson was to perform in Sydney, Australia, and then board a jet to carry out a second engagement in Hawaii on the same day. The jury awarded Abram $5.3 million in damages against Jackson. *See* http://www.cnn.com/2002/LAW/03/13/jackson.lawsuit.

Promoters must also deal with the expectations of fans. When one well-known R &

B artist walked onto a concert stage, sniffed around, declared "I don't like the audience," and then left, the promoter refunded the ticket costs to the audience.

Refunds become a thorny issue when the artist does actually play but gives an unsatisfactory performance. In *Kass v. Young*, one of the 14,000 patrons at a rock concert sued Neil Young because he terminated the concert by abruptly walking off the stage. 67 Cal. App. 3d 100, 136 Cal. Rptr. 469 (Cal. Ct. App. 1977). Kass sought to certify a class of all 14,000 present and retrieve their money.

The district court certified the class and awarded damages of $91,000 representing the cost of tickets purchased and a 40% attorney's fee. On appeal, the court vacated the judgment. It questioned whether all 14,000 patrons were equally damaged. The court postulated that "many of the patrons or 'fans' of the performer who had entertained them for an hour did not regard themselves cheated or that some may have sympathized with his antagonism toward a number of the security guards." *Id.* at 106-107. The court ruled that Kass' individual case could proceed following final determination of the class action.

Sometimes the misbehavior of musicians, their representatives, or even their fans places promoters in uncomfortable positions. Electric Factory Concerts (EFC), the local promoter of The Who concert at the Cincinnati Riverfront

Coliseum on December 3, 1979, was among the many defendants sued for wrongful death. A delay in opening up the concert doors led fans to rush in and trample several individuals to death. The appeals court found that EFC had received a permit to use and occupy the arena from 8:00 p.m. to 11:00 p.m. on December 3, 1979. *See* Bowes v. Cincinnati Riverfront Coliseum, 12 Ohio App.3d 12, 21, 465 N.E. 2d 904 (Ohio Ct. App. 1983).

By the permit, EFC was required to have a prescribed number of security and safety personnel in attendance. The court also found that the general manger and office manager for EFC was present on December 3rd and was a key person in determining when the doors would open. The court then reversed the trial court's order dismissing punitive damage claims against EFC. *Id.* at 23.

Since tragic incidents have taken place at several concerts, promoters have increased security. At one Snoop Dogg concert,[16] fans entered through doors pasted with signs reading "No Weapons Allowed" and "No Gang Activity Permitted Inside." They then encountered metal detectors and were subjected to security pat downs. While guards removed weapons, they did not confiscate drugs. After the leader of the

---

[16] *See* Sherri Burr, *Snoop Dogg, Schwartz Bob: Now that's a Full Evening*, ALBUQUERQUE TRIBUNE, Sept. 27, 2001.

warm-up band mounted the stage, he asked the crowd, "Where's the dope? Who's got the dope?"

"Over here, over here," the crowd responded as hundreds of hands shot up.

Whether it was the cloud of marijuana smoke or the deafening sounds, one patron fainted and had to be evacuated on a gurney. No lawsuits were later announced as a result of this concert. Some fans apparently have decided that they pay their money and take their chances with these kinds of events, a fortunate result for the local promoter.

C. MUSICIANS AND INDEBTEDNESS

For centuries, prominent musicians have been known to experience money troubles. Sometimes their indebtedness arises from poor management of substantial resources. At other times, the musicians overestimate their anticipated revenues from their recording, tour, and music publishing contracts. The result is that musicians, more than other entertainers, are more likely to have confrontations with creditors and the IRS. Attorneys who focus their practice on music law must enhance their knowledge of bankruptcy and tax law.

Wolfgang Amadeus Mozart earned more than double what he estimated it would cost a reputable family to survive in Vienna in the late 1700s, yet he routinely sent out begging letters to supplement his income. Peter Gay, *supra* note 14, at "Chapter 5. The Beggar." In seeking a path to the esteem of the nobility, Mozart wanted to appear as a cultivated artist and an equal, rather than as a hired hand. He spent considerable amounts on luxurious living quarters, paying in Vienna more than triple the amount he shelled out for a modest apartment in Salzburg. Biographer Peter Gay wrote, "What he craved he bought." Among other things, he purchased a specially built piano, prepared for tours with expensive handmade shoes and fashionable clothes, and acquired a billiard table. For his comfort, he kept a horse and deemed a carriage a necessity. *Id.*

To cover the additional cost associated with his extravagant lifestyle, Mozart wrote his friends and supporters. To one he said, "I beg you to help me with only a little money." He even requested that one associate lend him a substantial amount of money at an appropriate rate of interest so that he could secure a "sense of safety." He wrote, "It is nasty, indeed impossible, to live when one has to wait earnings to earnings." Mozart felt he needed "a certain serenity to do his composing." *Id.*

Some contemporary musicians could easily sympathize with Mozart's plight because they live from royalty check to royalty check. Part of the current problem is that musicians do not understand their recording contracts before signing them and therefore misperceive their potential earnings. Once their album or single sells at the gold, platinum, or diamond level, which are 500,000, 1,000,000, 10,000,000 units respectively, musicians expect the funds to pour in. In anticipation, they buy on credit a Cadillac SUV or full-size Mercedes, the equivalent of Mozart's carriage and horse.

Rap star MC Hammer built an elaborate home just prior to going bankrupt in the mid-1990s. Acknowledging that he had his priorities out of order, Hammer later became a minister. He was among the many musicians to find their coffers empty despite tremendous success.

When Mozart's creditors demanded payment, he begged for funds from others to pay them, constantly juggling his debt. *Id.* Modern musicians accomplish the same outcome by using one credit card to pay another. After Motown sued them, the Isley Brothers mentioned at their trial that they were having trouble making ends meet and initially planned to use the money Motown advanced them to pay bills and buy Christmas presents. While the jury believed them, the judge did not and ruled for Motown. *See* Isley v. Motown Record Corp., 69 F.R.D. 12 (S.D.N.Y. 1975).

Presently, musicians seek relief from their debts and contracts in bankruptcy court. Recording companies challenge the Chapter 11 filings by musicians, charging that they seek to be released from their agreements in bad faith. The bankruptcy court then examines the situation to determine if there is genuine financial distress.

James Taylor, the former lead singer of Kool and the Gang, was able to reject his executory contracts with PolyGram Records and two other publishing companies after filing for bankruptcy. *See* In re Taylor, 103 B.R. 511 (Bankr. D.N.J. 1989). The group arranged its recording, publishing, and tour related contracts and legal relationships through at least three furnishing companies. By October 1986, Kool and the Gang had accumulated debts exceeding $1,719,000. By December 1987, the group had outstanding loans and accounts totaling $3,352,109, which did not include another $950,000 advanced by PolyGram. Taylor, who petitioned for Chapter 11 bankruptcy relief on May 24, 1988, had personally guaranteed over $1.2 million of these loans. He also filed a motion for authority to reject certain executory agreements.

The recording and publishing companies filed a cross-motion seeking dismissal of Taylor's Chapter 11 petition for having been filed in bad faith. The court disagreed with the recording companies' claim. The court examined Taylor's financial situation and noted that his liabilities of $4,518,701.50 far exceeded his assets totaling only $734,215.00. *Id.* at 521. In affirming the decision of the Bankruptcy Court, the court observed that three contingent liabilities totaling over $1.2 million alone were sufficient to justify bankruptcy. *Id.* As a consequence, Taylor was able to reject his contracts and receive a "fresh start." *Id.* at 517.

The singing group TLC, which posted four No. 1 singles on Billboard's Hot 100 chart that sold 21 million albums in the United States alone, used a Chapter 11 bankruptcy filing to reject their existing management agreements. When the creditors charged bad faith, the court found that they too were financially distressed. The three women who comprised TLC had borrowed substantial sums totaling $349,922.26 from LaFace Records in March 1995. Their indebtedness was evidenced by demand promissory notes, which were to be payable from royalties. *See* In re Watkins, 210 B.R. 394, 395 (Bankr. N.D.Ga. 1997).

TLC used their LaFace loans to catch up on delinquent bills. Each woman testified that her financial problems had begun as early as 1994. All of them had difficulties meeting monthly payments and were constantly behind in paying their debts. Sometimes they were more than three months in arrears. Their December 31, 1994 royalty statement, which was received prior to their filing for bankruptcy, reflected a negative balance of $576,828.98.

One woman had credit card companies demanding payment, and couldn't pay her bills from month-to-month. When asked how the three came to the decision to file for relief, band member Rozonda Thomas stated that "[we pulled] out our pockets with nothing in them. That is exactly how we decided. None of us could pay our bills." *Id.* at 398-399.

Lisa Lopes, who would later die in a car wreck in Honduras at the age of 30, testified that she faced foreclosure on her Diamond Circle property, and two other creditors had sued her. *Id.* at 399. The court considered TLC's financial situation sufficiently dire to justify bankruptcy relief. *Id.* at 403. After their bankruptcy filing, TLC went on a five-year hiatus before releasing "Fanmail," their hit that sold more than 6 million copies.

Concerned about the increasing number of musicians filing for bankruptcy, the Recording Industry of Association America lobbied for an addition to the 1998 bankruptcy bill to make it harder for musicians to declare legal insolvency and escape their contracts. Their efforts fizzled out. Filing for bankruptcy remains an option for musicians seeking to escape their debts and oppressive contracts.

Even when musicians have sufficient funds coming in, some of them forget to pay their taxes. When the IRS sued country music singer and songwriter Willie Nelson and his wife Connie for failure to pay $1,514,752 in income taxes for the years 1975-1978, he petitioned to seal his records so his tax problems would not leak to the media and the general public. Willie Nelson Music Co. v. C.I.R., 85 T.C. 914 (Tax Ct. 1985).

The Nelsons claimed that sensationalism of their tax problems was causing them "undue embarrassment and considerable emotional distress." *Id.* at 916. They also claimed they had been "unable to negotiate large up front payments in long term endorsement contracts." *Id.*

The court examined 37 newspaper articles and concluded that none of them suggested that the Nelsons were subject to criminal prosecution. Rather, the newspapers gave a factual report on Nelsons' tax situation and none said that part of the underpayment was due to fraud. *Id.* at 925-926.

The court concluded that the Nelsons had not demonstrated sufficient good cause to seal the records and denied their motions. Historically, courts have sealed records where patents, trade secrets, or confidential information is involved. *Id.* at 921. This court said that showing the information "would harm a party's reputation is generally not sufficient to overcome the strong common law presumption in favor of access to court records." *Id.*

Nearly 20 years later, Nelson himself reminded the public of his tax problems by plugging H & R Block in television commercials during tax season.

The moral of this tale is that lawyers should encourage their musician clients to pay their taxes and refrain from buying a SUV, the modern equivalent of Mozart's carriage and horse, until they have the royalty check in hand.

CHAPTER 4

CENSORSHIP

Censorship in the entertainment industry has taken many forms as individuals and governments have sought to prohibit public exposure to material deemed politically, sexually, or violently offensive. Governments have blacklisted entertainers accused of supporting Communism and enacted mandatory and voluntary ratings codes. Throughout history, individuals and groups have banned and burned books, boycotted films and television programs, and labeled music as containing offensive, brutal lyrics. More recently, groups have targeted interactive games and the Internet for containing distasteful material. For their pains to eliminate the repulsive from public view, censoring groups have often just brought the items and their creators more attention and/or revenue.

Consider the following three examples.

Before its scheduled release date on February 25, 2004, Mel Gibson's *The Passion of Christ* became the subject of boycott calls from individuals who thought the film anti-Semitic and harsh toward Jews. *The Passion of Christ*, which cost $25 million to make, earned $23.6 million on its opening day and $295.3 million during its first 26 days at the box office, making it the highest grossing "R" rated film in history. Within 145 days, *The Passion of Christ* grossed $370,257,518 in the United States and over $500 million worldwide.

Similarly, African-American leaders called for a boycott of *The Barbershop* because of one character's irreverent comments toward famed Civil Rights leaders Rosa Parks, Dr. Martin Luther King Jr., and the Reverend Jesse Jackson. After *The Barbershop* grossed $75.8 million in 2002, the producers released *Barbershop 2: Back in Business* in 2004. With no boycott urged, the second one took in less revenue ($65,111,277) than the first.

In May 2004, The Walt Disney Corporation blocked its subsidiary Miramax from distributing the Michael Moore documentary *Fahrenheit 911* because it harshly criticized President Bush during an election year. *Fahrenheit 911* links President Bush to prominent Saudi Arabians, including the family of Osama bin Laden. It criticizes the President's actions before and after the Sept. 11th terrorist attacks. Although Disney and Miramax have a contractual agreement that allows Disney to prevent Miramax from distributing films under certain circumstances, such as an excessive budget or an NC-17 rating, Miramax claimed that neither applied to *Fahrenheit 911*. Disney acknowledged that it was apprehensive that the film might endanger tax breaks for its theme parks, hotels and other ventures in Florida, where the president's brother, Jeb, is governor. Miramax bought back Disney's share and contracted with Lion's Gate and IFC to distribute the film. Released on June 25, 2004, *Fahrenheit 911* became the weekend's #1 film, and promptly earned $93,984,261 million during its first 26 days, putting it on track to become the first documentary to gross over $100 million.

These three film examples are merely the tip of the censorship iceberg. This chapter first discusses the obscenity tests that western courts have developed over the last two centuries and then the specific efforts to ban books, films, music, and television programs from public view or rate their content.

A. OBSCENITY TESTS

In 1868, a British court declared that a pamphlet called "The Confessional Unmasked, shewing the depravity of the Romish priesthood, the iniquity of the Confessional, and the questions put to females in confession" to be obscene, an offence against the law of the land. *Regina v. Hicklin,* (1867-68) L.R. 3 Q.B. 360 (April 29, 1868). The *Hicklin* court asked, "whether the tendency of the matter charged as obscenity is to deprave and corrupt those whose minds are open to such immoral influences, and into whose hands a publication of this sort may fall?"

In applying its test to the "The Confessional Unmasked," the court declared that it would suggest to the young and old "thoughts of a most impure and libidinous character[,] ... thoughts and desires which otherwise would have not occurred to their minds."

In 1957, the United States Supreme Court rejected the *Hicklin* test as too restrictive of the freedoms of speech and press. In *Roth v. United States*, 354 U.S. 476 (1957), the Court declared that obscenity should not be judged by "the effect of isolated passages upon the most susceptible persons" as this "might well encompass material legitimately treating with sex."

Samuel Roth was convicted under a federal obscenity statute for mailing obscene circulars, advertising, and a book. The Court upheld Roth's conviction under the federal obscenity statute, which declared, "Every obscene, lewd, lascivious, or filthy book, pamphlet, picture, paper, letter, writing, print, or other publication of an indecent character ... [i]s declared to be nonmailable matter and shall not be conveyed in the mails or delivered from any post office or by any letter carrier."

Sixteen years later, the Supreme Court affirmed Roth's holding that "obscene material is not protected by the First Amendment, and pronounced the most comprehensive obscenity test in *Miller v. California*, 413 U.S. 15 (1973). The *Miller* Court requires a trier of fact to consider:

> (a) whether 'the average person, applying contemporary community standards' would find the work, taken as a whole, appeals to the prurient interest;
> (b) whether the work depicts or describes, in a patently offensive way, sexual conduct specifically defined by the applicable state law; and
> (c) whether the work, taken as a whole, lacks serious literary, artistic, political, or scientific value.

Marvin Miller was convicted under a California obscenity statute after having mailed brochures advertising four books entitled, "Intercourse," "Man-Woman," "Sex Orgies Illustrated," and "An Illustrated History of Pornography," and a film entitled 'Marital Intercourse" to a California restaurant. The manager of the restaurant and his mother opened the envelope.

The Court declared that "[s]ex and nudity may not be exploited without limit by films or pictures exhibited or sold in places of public accommodation any more than live sex and nudity can be exhibited or sold without limit in such public places." The court noted, nevertheless, that medical books may contain graphic illustrations and descriptions of human anatomy, but would not be deemed obscene.

Miller's conviction was vacated and remanded for further proceedings consistent with the new test.

In *Pope v. Illinois*, 481 U.S. 497 (1987), the Supreme Court addressed the third prong of the *Miller* test, and said "[t]he proper inquiry is not whether an ordinary member of any given community would find serious literary, artistic, political, or scientific value in allegedly obscene material, but whether a reasonable person would find such value in the material taken as a whole."

These obscenity tests have been applied to numerous entertainment materials as individuals or groups have sought to ban books, films, music, games, and television programs as obscene. The film, music, and television industries have responded with self-regulation by enacting ratings codes that alert potential purchasers or viewers that the material contained therein may give offense.

B. FILM CENSORSHIP

The film industry has been faced with efforts to censor movies for their political, sexual, and violent content. After World War II, filmmakers became subjected to political censorship. During the 1960s, states sought to censor certain films by imposing ratings codes. Beginning in the 1970s and continuing today, the Motion Picture Association of America, in an attempt to self-regulate, adopted rating categories (X, R, PG, G) to give viewers an indication of what to expect in terms of content. Each of these periods will be discussed herein, as well as more modern efforts to hold the media accountable when individuals emulate violent or tortious behavior that leads to the death of, or causes harm to, other innocent civilians.

1. THE MCCARTHY ERA

In 1938, the House of Representatives established its Un-American Activities Committee. In 1947, with the rise of the Cold War following World War II, this Committee announced a wide program to investigate Communist influences in Hollywood.

Congressional leaders, led by Wisconsin Senator Joseph McCarthy, became concerned that Communists had infiltrated the Hollywood film industry. As a result, a multitude of screenwriters, directors, and actors were blacklisted as suspected members of the Communist party, and had their careers nearly destroyed or ruined. Screenwriter Lillian Hellman, for example, wrote four films before being blacklisted in 1952. Subsequently, she wrote only one film, *The Chase*, which starred Marlon Brando, Robert Redford, and Jane Fonda. It premiered in 1966.

When screenwriters John Howard Lawson and Dalton Trumbo appeared before the House Committee on Un-American Activities, they refused, as did several other filmmakers, to answer whether they had been or were members of the Screen Actors Guild and of the Communist party. They were subsequently convicted under 2 U.S.C.A. § 192, which makes it a misdemeanor to refuse to answer the questions of a Congressional Committee. They argued on appeal in *Lawson v. United States*, 176 F.2d 49 (D.C. Cir. 1949), that the Bill of Rights protects citizens from being compelled to disclose their private beliefs and associations.

The District of Columbia Court of Appeals, however, disagreed with their assertions and affirmed their convictions. The court expressly held "that the House Committee on Un-American Activities, or a properly appointed subcommittee thereof, has the power to inquire whether a witness subpoenaed by it is or is not a member of the Communist Party or a believer in communism and that this power carries with it necessarily the power to effect criminal punishment for failure or refusal to answer that question under 2 U.S.C.A. § 192." The court held that the committee's power also included the right to inquire into membership into the Screen Actors Guild.

In 1962, eight screenwriters and four screen actors, who had been blacklisted, claimed that the Sherman Anti-trust laws prohibited seven motion picture producing and distributing companies and two motion picture trade associations from inquiring into their political associations and beliefs. In *Young v. Motion Picture Association of America,* 28 F.R.D. 2 (D.D.C. 1961), the filmmakers charged that the MPAA had circulated and published throughout the motion picture industry a "blacklist" containing the names of persons, including the plaintiffs, who were accused of Communist membership or affiliation.

Once the plaintiffs' names appeared on the blacklist, the plaintiffs claimed that defendants refused to distribute motion pictures utilizing their services, or refused to utilize their services except on a black market at greatly reduced prices. The plaintiffs also accused the defendants of maintaining an industry-wide clearance program that permitted the use of only those individuals whose names had been cleared.

Judge Walsh refused to declare that the activities of the defendants were *per se* unlawful under the Sherman Act. Walsh found that the defendants might have legitimate business interest in "(1) controlling the possible subversive Communist propaganda that the hiring of Communist Party members might introduce to the movie-going public, and (2) protecting their investment in the motion picture business from poor attendance or boycotting by the theatergoing public because of the employment therein of suspected members of the Communist Party. The case was affirmed in *Young v. Motion Picture Association of America,* 299 F.2d 119 (D.C.Cir. 1962).

Congress formerly abolished the House Committee on Un-American Activities in 1974.

2. STATE CENSORSHIP ORDNANCES

During the 1960s, states began enacting ordinances requiring the film industry to apply for permits, submit all motion pictures for examination prior to their public exhibition, and pay a license fee. When Time Film Corp, which owned the exclusive right to publicly exhibit *Don Juan* in Chicago, applied for its permit, it paid the license fee but refused to submit the film for examination. The permit was denied, and TFC sued claiming that the Chicago ordinance violated its First Amendment rights to free speech. The U.S. District Court dismissed the suit and the Court of Appeals affirmed.

In *Time Film Corp. v. City of Chicago,* 365 U.S. 43 (1961), the U.S. Supreme Court held that states and cities could require producers to submit their films in advance for a prior determination of whether they contained obscene material. The Court cited its holding in *Roth v. United States* that "obscenity is not within the area of constitutionally protected speech." The Court noted, however, that city officials do not have "the power to prevent the showing of any motion picture they deem unworthy of a license."

Nevertheless, when Ronald Freedman was convicted under a Maryland statute of exhibiting a film before submitting it to the board of censors, the Supreme Court overturned his conviction in *Freedman v. State of Maryland*, 380 U.S. 51 (1965), finding the Maryland statute too burdensome. When the case was argued in November 1964, only four states (Maryland, New York, Virginia, and Kansas) and four cities (Chicago, Detroit, Fort Worth and Providence) had active censorship laws. Twenty-eight municipalities had inactive ordinances.

In his concurrence in *Freedman*, Justice Douglas indicated the court was requiring that a movie censorship system contain at least three procedural safeguards if it is not to run afoul of the First Amendment: (1) the censor must have the burden of instituting judicial proceedings; (2) any restraint prior to judicial review can be imposed only briefly in order to preserve the status quo; and (3) a prompt judicial determination of obscenity must be assured. 380 U.S. at 62. Justice Douglas also stated that the Chicago censorship ordinance, upheld in *Times Film Corp*, would not survive these standards.

3. MPAA RATINGS CODES

The state censorship ordinances gave way to more stringent industry self-regulation in the late 1960s. The Motion Picture Association of America (MPAA), a New York not-for profit corporation, is composed of producers and distributors of motion pictures and television program. Right after former Lyndon Johnson aide Jack Valenti became the MPAA president in 1966,[17] controversy arose around the use of the word "screw" and the phrase "hump the hostess," along with the display of nudity in *Whose Afraid of Virginia Woolf.*

To resolve this controversy, the MPAA banded together with other industry groups to create four ratings codes that would give parents advance cautionary warnings so they could make informed decisions about the movies their young children see. In 1968, the initial four categories were "G for General Audiences;" "M for mature audiences;" "R for restricted to Parents who must accompany children;" and "X for no one under 17 admitted." The "M" rating was later changed to "PG: Parental Guidance Suggested" because some parents regarded "M" as sterner than "R."

---

[17] Valenti's tenure continued for 38 years. On July 1, 2004, the MPAA announced that Dan Glickman, former secretary of Agriculture during the Clinton years, would succeed him. *See* Susan Crabtree, *Casting Against type: Glickman an unusual choice to top MPAA, available at* www.variety.com/index .asp?layout=print_story&articleid=VR1117907311%c ategory id=10. Crabtree wrote, "As the former U.S.' former ambassador of wheat and cattle, Glickman is also at ease negotiating international trade deals and traveling around the world seeking concessions from countries such as China, where piracy flourishes." *Id.*

Subsequently, the MPAA split the PG category into PG and PG-13 in 1984, and changed the X to NC-17 in 1990. Today, the MPAA rates movies in one of the following categories:

G--General Audiences. All ages admitted.

PG--Parental Guidance Suggested. Some material may not be suitable for children.

PG-13--Parents Strongly Cautioned. Some material may be inappropriate for children under 13.

R--Restricted. Under 17 requires accompanying parent or adult guardian.

NC-17--No one under 17 admitted.

The MPAA also rates movie trailers, which advertise coming attractions, as either approved for "all audiences," or "restricted audiences." If the trailer receives the latter tag, then it can only be advertised with feature films rated R or NC-17. According to director John Carlos Frey (*The Gatekeeper*), this makes a huge difference in the efforts to advertise movies. Frey re-cut his trailer to eliminate a scene where guns are raised towards the audience after it received a "restricted audience" rating.

On the MPAA website, www.mpaa.org, Jack Valenti states that the Rating Board, composed of 8 to 13 members located in Los Angeles, "does not rate movies on their quality or lack of quality." Rather, he writes that the "basic mission of the ratings system is a simple one: to offer to parents some advance information about movies so that parents can decide what movies they want their children to see or not to see." *Id.*

Producers/distributors must elect to submit their films to the Ratings Board. If they chose to forego a rating, they may market their films as not rated or in any way they prefer so long as, according to Valenti, "it is not confusing similar to the G, PG, PG-13, R, and NC-7. These ratings symbols are federally–registered certification marks of the MPAA and may not be self applied." *Id.*

Those producers/distributors who opt to submit their films for ratings and become unhappy with the results, may appeal the ratings to the Rating Appeals Board, comprised of 14 to 18 men and women from industry organizations that govern the ratings systems. By a two-thirds vote, the Ratings Appeals Board can overturn a Ratings Board decision.

Producers/distributors who remain unhappy with this result, may protest to the public or appeal to the court system. When the Ratings Appeals Board upheld the R rating given to *Fahrenheit 9/11*, Michael Moore encouraged "all teenagers to come see my movie, by any means necessary." He added, "If you need me to sneak you in, let me know." *See*

Gabriel Snyder, *MPAA going 'R' way on '9/11' rating*, VARIETY, *available at* http://www.variety.com/index.asp?layout=print_story&articleid=VR1117906845&categoryid=13.

Miramax Films Corp challenged the X rating given to director Pedro Almodovar's *Tie Me Up! Tie Me Down!* in court, claiming it was arbitrary and capricious conduct and requested a judicially imposed R rating. The Ratings Board unanimously accorded an X rating to the film because of two sexually explicit scenes and the visual depiction of sex acts. While Miramax and Almodovar were accorded an opportunity to delete or edit the objectionable scenes, they declined. They petitioned the Ratings Appeal Board for a review, but the Board upheld the X rating.

In *Miramax Films Corp v. MPAA*, 560 N.Y.S. 2d (1990), the New York Supreme Court declared that while the ratings system was "censorship from within the industry rather than imposed from without, but censorship nonetheless." It admonished that "the rating system's categories have been fashioned by the motion picture industry to create an illusion of concern for children, imposing censorship, yet all the while facilitating the marketing of exploitive and violent films with an industry seal of approval." The court, however, dismissed the petition and denied the requested relief to change the rating to an R because the court was not the appropriate vehicle to afford such relief.

In *Maljack Productions v. MPAA*, 52 F.3d 373 (D.C. Cir. 1995), and independent movie and video production company sued MPAA because of the X rating given to *Henry: Portrait of a Serial Killer* for its violent content. Maljack, which elected to distribute the film as un-rated, claimed that the picture was not as successful as it would have been had it received an R rating. Maljack alleged in its complaint that the MPPAA discriminated against it and gave the *Henry* film an X rating because Maljack was not a MPAA member.

The district court dismissed the complaint for failure to state a claim, but the Court of Appeals for the District of Columbia Circuit overturned the dismissal and remanded. The court said that if the MPAA had indeed given *Henry* an X rating because Maljack was not a member, then it breached its implied covenant of good faith and fair dealing.

While the X ratings generated controversy, the R rating has also led to lawsuits. In *Borger by Borger v. Bisciglia*, 888 F. Supp. 97 (E.D. Wis. 1995), a 16-year-old sued the Kenosha School District and its superintendent for refusing to allow *Schindler's List*, an R rated film, to be shown as part of his high school curriculum. The superintendent rejected several history teachers' request to take their students to a local theatre to see *Schindler's List* because it was R rated. The school board's policy dictated that "no films having a rating of R, NC-

17, or X shall be shown to students at any school."

The court in *Borger* noted that while "Students do not lose their First Amendment rights when they walk through the schoolhouse door," the School Board can use "the ratings system as a filter of films." In dismissing Bolger's motions for summary judgment, the court further stated that the School Board established that the MPAA rings are "a reasonable way of determining which movies are more likely to contain harsh language, nudity, and inappropriate material for high school students."

4. FILM VIOLENCE

Critics have often charged, as in the cases above, that the MPAA is more likely to censor for explicit sex that violence.   The violent content of films has become even more of a concern as individuals have imitated certain films' dangerous acts and caused great bodily harm or even death to others.

In *Yakubowich v. Paramount Pictures*, 536 N.E. 2d, 1067 (Mass. S. Ct. 1989), William Yakubovitch sued Paramount Pictures and the Saxon Theatre Corporation charging that they were responsible for the knifing death of their son. A Saxon Theater patron, Michael Barrett, watched Paramount's film *The Warriors*, which depicts juvenile gang-related violence, before killing Martin Yakubowicz.

William Yakubowich claimed that Paramount and Saxon Theater should be held liable for his son's death on both negligence and First Amendment Grounds. The court found that the defendants did not violated their duty of reasonable care and that the film was protected on First Amendment grounds. When Yakubowich raised the "incitement" exception, which applies to speech that advocates "the use of force: or incites or produces "imminent lawless action." However, the court noted that speech does not lose its First Amendment protection merely because it has "a tendency to lead to violence." *Id.*

The court found that the fictional film does not "at any point exhort, urge, entreat, solicit, or overtly advocate or encourage unlawful or violent activity on the part of viewers." *Id.* The court held that Paramount did not act unreasonably in producing, distributing and exhibiting the film, nor did Saxon Theater act unreasonably in exhibiting it. Since the killing took place several miles from the theater, Paramount did not fail to take reasonable steps to warn patrons and Saxon did not fail to exercise proper supervision. The court placed Barrett's killing of Yakubowicz squarely on Barrett's shoulders.

A film that generated even more concern for its violent content was *Natural Born Killers*. Sarah Edmondson and her boyfriend Benjamin Darrus watched *Natural Born Killers* over and over again the night before they went on a shooting spree, during which they shot Patsy Byers and rendered her a paraplegic, and then murdered William Savage. In *Byers v. Edmondson*, 826 So. 2d 551 (La. Ct. App. 2002). Patsy Byers sued Edmondson along with Time Warner and Oliver Stone, the director of *Natural Born Killers*, for damages related to her injuries. The court granted the motion to dismiss the actions against Stone and Warner because it found *Natural Born Killers* to be protected speech.

Byers alleged that the film was not entitled to First Amendment protection because it was either inciteful or obscene, but the court disagreed. While the court acknowledged that *Natural Born Killers* was permeated with violent imagery, the violence was fictionalized and does not "order or command anyone to perform any concrete action immediately or at any specific time." The court also noted that Byers failed to allege that *Natural Born Killers* met the three *Miller* test criteria to be judged obscene. In *State v. Johnson*, 343 So.2d 705, 709-10 (La. 1977), the Louisiana Supreme Court noted that "The First Amendment does not permit a violence-based notion of obscenity."

C. TELEVISION CENSORSHIP

Should television networks be mandated to portray only those shows that do not offend the sensitivities of the American populace? Most people would say no, although many think there should be a warning system. Because of this concern, private and public institutions have adopted ratings to alert Americans as to the programming content appearing on their small screens.

For the most part, the broadcast industry self-regulates to keep indecent programming from appearing on the airwaves at inappropriate times. In 1996, Congress asked the industry to establish a voluntary ratings system[18] for TV programs to alert parents about the material their children watch. The National Association of Broadcasters, the National Cable Television Association, and the Motion Picture Association of America collaborated to establish six ratings codes, which appear on the screen during the first 15 seconds of each television program.

TV-Y	(All Children)
TV-7	(Directed to Older Children)
TV-G	(General Audience)
TV-PG	(Parental Guidance Suggested)
TV-14	(Parents Strongly Cautioned)
TV-MA	(Mature Audience Only)

The first three ratings are directed solely towards children. The TV-Y (All Children) designation means that the show is appropriate for all children. It is found only on children's

---

[18] A complete description of the ratings system is available thorough the FCC website, which is accessible at www.fcc.gov. This chapter contains only a succinct summary of the system and how it is meant to work.

shows. The TV-7 (Directed to Older Children) label is also only attached to children's shows. TV-7 indicates the show is most appropriate for children age 7 and older. TV-G (General Audience) marks the program as suitable to all ages, although it may not be a children's show.

The TV-PG (Parental Guidance Suggested) tag is similar to its film equivalent, PG. It suggests that parents decide whether the material is suitable for younger children. TV-PG may also be accompanied by a V for violence, an S for sexual situations, an L for language, or a D for suggestive dialogue.

The final two ratings are TV-14 (Parents Strongly Cautioned) and TV-MA (Mature Audience Only). The first rating indicates a show that may be unsuitable for children under 14. The V, S, L, and D labels associated with TV-PG may also accompany TV-14. The rating TV-MA suggests a show that is unsuitable for children under 17 as the program may contain explicit sexual content.

A TV Parental Guidelines Monitoring Board--composed of members from the broadcast and cable television industry, the program production community, and the advocacy— scrutinizes the application of these ratings to make sure they are being applied accurately and consistently. Any parent or other member of the general public can protest a rating they believed to be misapplied.

To aid parents in applying these ratings codes within their homes, the Federal Communications Commission requires all television sets 13 inches or larger contain V-chip technology if manufactured after January 1, 2000. The V-Chip allows parents to block their children from watching certain programming. Since the V-chip reads the ratings, parents can use a remote control to keep certain programs from appearing on their screens.

1. FCC INDECENCY REGULATIONS

The Federal Communications Commission's oversight over television extends to enforcing the federal law that forbids the broadcast of obscene material and limits the showing of indecent and profane television. The FCC follows the *Miller* three-part definition of obscenity that is prohibited by the First Amendment. The FCC defines indecency as

"language or material that, in context, depicts or describes, in terms patently offensive as measured by contemporary community broadcast standards for the broadcast medium, sexual or excretory organs or activities."[19]

The FCC defines profanity as language that:

---

[19]   *See*   http://www.fcc.gov/cgb/consumerfacts/ obscene.html

"denote[s] certain of those personally reviling epithets naturally tending to provoke violent resentment or denoting language so grossly offensive to members of the public who actually hear it as to amount to a nuisance."

Id. Because indecent and profane speech programming does not rise to the level of obscenity, they benefit from First Amendment protection.

Rather than banning indecent programming and profane speech entirely from television and radio broadcasts, the FCC limits such material to the hours of 10:01 p.m. to 5:59 a.m. The FCC prohibits indecent programming and profane speech between the hours of 6:00 a.m. and 10:00 p.m.

Even with these limits, the ratings system, and V-chip technology in place, sometimes the general public may be exposed to material they deem indecent during primetime. Several hundreds of thousands of individuals complained bitterly to the FCC after Janet Jackson and Justin Timberlake performed a song and dance routine for the Feb. 1, 2004, Super Bowl half-time show. At the end of the routine, Timberlake sang the lyrics, "I gotta have you naked by the end of this song," as he tore off part of Jackson's top and exposed her bejeweled right breast for almost two seconds.

The performance had personal consequences for both singers. Janet Jackson was dropped from starring in an ABC television movie based on the life of Lena Horne after Horne refused to cooperate with the production as long as Jackson remained in the role. See Lawrence Van Gelder, *Art Briefing*, N.Y. TIMES, Feb. 26, 2004. Timberlake cancelled his commitment to co-host ABC's Motown 45 special with Lionel Richie after a coalition of African-American organizations protested the Timberlake connection. *Id.*

Further, the Senate voted to increase fines tenfold to $275,000 per indecency violation, up to a maximum of $3 million. The House Energy and Commerce Committee mulled over an amendment to require the FCC to hold hearings on whether to revoke a broadcaster's license after three indecency violations. Reuters, *Senate Panel to Consider New Indecency Bill—McCain*, N.Y. TIMES, Mar. 2, 2004.

After the Senate bill passed, FCC chairman Michael Powell proposed fining Viacom, CBS's parent company, $275,000 a second for each of the two seconds Jackson's breast appeared on television. The FCC fine only applied to the 16 TV stations directly owned and operated by Viacom. In 2004, the FCC also issued a record fine of $1.75 million against Clear Channel, for indecency complaints against Howard Stern and other radio personalities.[20]

In an effort to address sexually oriented programming on cable television, Congress passed Section 505 of the Telecommunications Act of 1996. It required cable television operators who provide channels "primarily dedicated to sexually-oriented programming" either to "fully scramble or otherwise fully block" those channels or to limit their transmission to hours when children are unlikely to be viewing, such as between 10:00 p.m. and 6:00 a.m. *See* United States v. Playboy Entertainment Group, 529 U.S. 803, 806 (2000).

Although cable companies use scrambling in the regular course of business, scrambling can be imprecise leading to "signal bleed." The Supreme Court observed that the purpose of § 505 was to shield children from hearing or seeing images resulting from signal bleed. *Id.*

To comply with § 505, cable operators adopted a "time channeling" approach, in which they eliminated the transmission of targeted programming outside the safe harbor period. Playboy challenged § 505 as "unnecessarily

---

[20] *See* Jube Shiver Jr., *2 seconds of breast could cost CBS $550,000, available at* http://www.sfgate.com/cgi-bin/article.cgi?file=/chronicle/archive/2004/07/01/MNGKI7ES7B1.DTL.

restrictive content-based legislation violative of the First Amendment." *Id.* at 807.

The Supreme Court agreed and affirmed the district court's prior ruling declaring that § 505 violates the First Amendment. The court noted that unlike, broadcast networks, cable television systems had the capacity to block unwanted channels on a household-by-household basis. This "targeted blocking enables the Government to support parental authority without affecting the First Amendment interests of speakers and willing listeners." *Id.* at 815. Since target blocking is less restrictive than banning, the Court concluded, "the Government cannot ban speech if target blocking is a feasible and effective means of furthering its compelling interests." *Id.*

2. TELEVISION VIOLENCE

In addition to complaining to Congress and the FCC, individuals have sued network broadcasters for showing violence on television that they believed led to tortious and/or criminal behavior. In *Graves v. Warner Brothers*, the parents of Scott Amedure sued *The Jenny Jones Show*, charging that one of its programs led to the death of their son. 253 Mich. App. 486, 656 N.W.2d 195 (Mich. Ct. App. 2002).

On a show about secret crushes, Scott Amedure was invited to reveal his previously undisclosed affections towards Jonathan Schmitz. Three days after the taping, Amedure left a sexually charged note on Schmitz's front door. Schmitz bought a 12-gauge pump-action shotgun, drove to Amedure's home, and fatally shot him in the chest. Schmitz was convicted of second-degree murder and sentenced to a prison term of twenty-five to fifty years.

Amedure's parents sought to lay the blame for Schmitz's behavior on *The Jenny Jones Show*, its producer, and owner. Amedure's parents argued that by intentionally withholding from Schmitz that the true topic of the show was same-sex crushes, the defendants knew or should have known that their actions would incite violence, with the sole purpose of increasing their ratings. A jury found in favor of Amedure's parents and awarded $29,332,686 in damages.

On appeal the judgment was reversed and vacated. The Michigan Court of Appeals determined that *The Jenny Jones Show* did not owe a duty to protect Amedure from harm caused by Schmitz. The court said, "[T]here is no legal duty obligating one person to aid or protect another.... Moreover, an individual has no duty to protect another from the criminal acts of a third party in the absence of a special relationship." *Id.* at 493. The court observed, "[c]riminal activity, by its deviant nature, is normally unforeseeable." *Id.*

The court decided that *The Jenny Jones Show* "had no duty to anticipate and prevent the act of murder committed by Schmitz three days after leaving defendant's studio and hundreds of miles away." *Id.* at 497. The court perceived the relationship between *The Jenny Jones Show* and Schmitz as one of business invitor to invitee and that ended after the taping on March 6, 1995, three days before the murder. On March 6, both men peacefully left the studio. *Id.*

The Jenny Jones Show never aired the March 6 episode. On June 21, 2004, the United States Supreme Court denied the parents' request for a writ of certiorari, thus ending their appeals.

In an incident from the 1970s, teenagers attacked another adolescent after observing a brutal scene on the NBC drama "Born Innocent." In the television movie, four girls violently raped an adolescent girl with a plumber. In the real life incident, a nine-year-old girl was attacked on the beach.

Olivia N. sued NBC, claiming that the television show incited the violence against her. *Olivia N. v. NBC*, 74 Cal.App.3d 383, 141 Cal. Rptr. 511 (Cal. Ct. App. 1977). After reviewing the entire film, the trial judge determined that it did not advocate or encourage violent and depraved acts, and entered judgment for the defendants. The California Appeals Court overturned the ruling, and ordered the trial court to impanel a jury and proceed to trial. *Id.*

On remand, Olivia N's counsel admitted that he couldn't prove incitement in his opening statement. This led the trial court to grant NBC's motion for a nonsuit. When the counsel appealed that decision, the California Court of Appeal affirmed the judgment. *See* Olivia N. v. NBC, 126 Cal. App.3d 488, 178 Cal. Rptr. 888 (Cal. Ct. App. 1981). NBC was thus able to stop a full trial on the merits of Olivia N's case.

D. MUSIC CENSORSHIP

This section discusses music ratings, music violence, and issues concerning community standards.

1. MUSIC RATINGS & VIOLENCE

The music industry has the simplest ratings system of all. Either the producer or distributor will stamp the CD, LP or cassette with the designation:

"Parental advisory: explicit content."

That alert, however, is not sufficient to stop individuals from suing songwriters, singers, producers, and distributors over music believed to cause death.

In *McCollum v. CBS*, the parents of John Daniel McCollum sued John "Ozzy" Osbourne," CBS Records and other individuals and companies for composing, performing, producing, and distributing an album they alleged caused the death of their son John. 202 Cal. App. 3d 989, 249 Cal.Rptr. 187 (Cal. Ct. App. 1988). Among the songs John listened to the night before shooting himself in the temple was "Suicide Solution," with the lyrics "suicide is the only way out." He was found wearing headphones with the stereo still running. *Id.* at 995.

While John's parents alleged that it was foreseeable that Osbourne's music would influence peculiarly susceptible individuals to act in a manner destructive to their person or body, the court disagreed. The court concluded that the First Amendment protected Osbourne's music. In order to constitute culpable incitement, the court said Osbourne's music must be (1) directed and intended toward the goal of bringing about the imminent suicide of listeners and (2) likely to produce such a result. After finding that Osbourne's music met neither test, the court ruled that Osbourne and the other defendants bore no responsibility for John's suicide. *Id.* at 1000-1001.

In a 1990 interview, Osbourne said, "If I wrote music for people who shot themselves after listening to my music, I wouldn't have much of a following.[21] Nevertheless, Osbourne was sued again when another individual Michael Jeffery Waller committed suicide after

---

[21]   http://rockonthenet.com/artists-o/ozzyosbourne.htm.

repeatedly listening to his music. Waller's parents claimed the song "Suicide Solution" contained subliminal messages. The district court ruled, and the court appeals affirmed that Osbourne's First Amendment rights protected him from being held liable for claims of negligence, nuisance, fraud, and invasion of privacy. *Waller v. Osbourne*, 763 F.Supp. 1144 (M.D.Ga. 1991), *aff'd*, 958 F.2d 1084 (11th Cir. 1992).

In a different case, Ronald Howard attempted to avoid the death penalty by claiming that listening to "2Pacalypse Now" caused him to shoot Officer Bill Davidson. One song on the album contained the following lyrics: "My brain locks, my Glock's like a f--kin mop; The more I shot, the more mothaf--ka's dropped; And even cops got shot when they rolled up." *Id.* at *1. The jury apparently did not believe that these lyrics were enough to cause someone to shoot a police officer because it sentenced Howard to death. *Id.*

When the relatives of officer Davidson sued Tupac Shakur, Interscope Records, and Time Warner, they also claimed the album was responsible for the offer's death. The court disagreed, finding the album protected by the First Amendment. The court observed that while Shakur's words offend, they "are not 'by their very nature' likely to cause violence." Further, the court said, "no reasonable jury could conclude that persons would reflexively lash out because of the language of Shakur's recording."

Moreover, "Ronald Howard did not reflexively react based on Shakur's offensive speech." *Id.* at 18.

Even when the music industry is charged with targeting minors with violent lyrics, courts have been reluctant to allow lawsuits to proceed on First Amendment grounds. Fifteen-year old Elyse Pahler was kidnapped, tortured, raped and murdered by three adolescent males who said they planned to emulate the band Slayer. When her parents sued the band and their recording and distributing companies, the court dismissed the case of *Pahler v. Slayer*, 2001 WL 1736476 (Cal. Superior Ct 2001). The court stated, "Unless the products are harmful to children or incite imminent unlawful conduct, no statute or regulation specifically prohibits or restricts the sale or distribution of Slayer albums to children." *Id.* at *2.

These cases indicate the importance of parents paying attention to the music rating "Parental advisory: explicit content." Parents should preview the music before permitting their children to purchase particular albums. If the child already owns a substantial collection through gifts or purchase, parents should monitor all of their acquisitions to determine if their kids are listening to violently or sexually charged lyrics and confiscate the music if necessary.

Suing the music industry after they have lost their children not only doesn't bring them back, but also the parents may receive no compensation for their loss if they are unable to maintain their lawsuit. These cases demonstrate that the First Amendment is a large hurdle to clear. Short of the music actually giving explicit instructions on how to commit murder, suicide, or other violent crimes, *see Rice v. Paladin Enterprises*, 128 F.3d 233 (4th Cir. 1997), the parents may have no recourse against the industry. Policing the industry begins at home.

2. COMMUNITY STANDARDS

The first prong of the *Miller* test requires the court to apply contemporary community standards to determine whether the work, taken as a whole, appeals to prurient interest as part of determining whether it is obscene. At least one judge considered himself as a fitting representative of his community.

When a Broward county sheriff discouraged record stores from selling the album "As Nasty as They Wanna Be," the musicians filed suit to enjoin the sheriff from interfering with record sales. The district court granted the injunction, but declared the song obscene. Skyywalker Records, Inc. v. Navarro, 739 F.Supp. 578, (S.D.Fla. 1990).

The court of appeals found two problems with the case. First, the court noted the sheriff put in no evidence other than "Nasty As They Wanna Be" tape recording, while the plaintiffs put in substantial evidence concerning the three-part Miller test. *See* Luke Records v. Navarro, 960 F.2d 134, 136 (11th Cir. 1992).

Second, court of appeals expressed concern that the district judge tried the case without a jury, relying on his own expertise. The district judge determined that the relevant community was Broward, Dade, and Palm Beach Counties. He stated that he had resided in Broward County since 1958, had practiced law and been a judge in the community, and had personal knowledge of this area's demographics, culture, economics, and politics. He had attended public functions and events in all three counties and is aware of the community's concerns as reported in the media and by word of mouth. The judge also mentioned his personal knowledge of the nature of obscenity in the community obtained from viewing dozens, if not hundreds of allegedly obscene films and other publications seized by law enforcement. *Id.* at 137.

The court of appeals said that it is difficult to review the value judgments of the judge as fact finder. In reversing, the court of appeals stated that the sheriff failed to meet his burden of proving that the recording is obscene because he submitted no evidence to contradict the testimony that the work had artistic value. The court concluded, "A work cannot be held obscene unless each element of the Miller test has been met. We reject the argument that simply by listening to this musical work, the judge could determine that it had no serious artistic value." *Id.* at 137-138.

E. GAME & INTERNET RATINGS

This chapter concludes with a brief reference to efforts to rate the Internet and interactive video games played on GameBoy, Nintendo, Play Station, Xbox and other systems.

The Internet Content Rating Association (ICRA), an international, independent organization, regulates the Internet. It claims to empower parents to make informed decisions about electronic media by openly and objectively labeling the Internet's content. *See* http://www.icra.org/_en/about. ICRA says it aims simultaneously to protect children from potentially harmful material and free speech on the Internet. *Id.* Once an Internet provider has answered the ICRA questionnaire about the sexual nature, violence content, abusive language, and use of alcohol, tobacco, and drugs, ICRA generate a label indicating the content of the cite.

An Electronic Software Ratings Board applies five ratings to interactive video games. Manufacturers voluntarily submit their games.

eC: early childhood
E: everyone
T: teen
M: mature
Ao: adults only

The designation "eC: early childhood" indicates a game appropriate for ages 3 and up; "E: everyone" can be used by ages 6 and up; "T: teen" should be purchased only for ages 13 and order; "M: mature" should be reserve for ages 17 and older; and "Ao: adults only" should only be bought and played by adults. The Electronic Software Ratings Board assigns these designations based on a submitted tape and questionnaire. *Id.* at 132.

The interactive game industry also uses phrases such as animated violence, comic mischief, strong language, and mature sexual themes to refer to its content. *Id.* Bushman and Cantor report, "According to the Interactive Digital Software Association's Website (http://www.idsa.com), 71% of video game titles are rated E (everyone), 19% are rated T (teen), and 7% are rated M (mature). *Id.* at 133. The website also reports that "Sixty-five percent of parents with children under the age of 18 say that computer and video games are a positive addition to their children's lives." *See* http://www.theesa.com/press room.html.

While all ratings might be considered a form of censorship, they are all voluntary. The ultimate goal is to guide parents in making decisions about the content of the entertainment that their children experience. The entertainment industry is putting the onus on the parents to be the final determinant.

When surveyed by the Kaiser Foundation, parents were asked to report on their reaction to the various industry ratings. Fifty-three percent found movie ratings very useful and 40% classified them as useful. For television, 48% found the television ratings very useful, and 44% said they were useful. For music 52% of parents found the single rating very useful and 40% somewhat useful. Interactive games received a similar reaction, with 52% finding the ratings very useful and 41% finding them somewhat useful. [22] This indicates that the overwhelming majority of parents find industry ratings helpful.

---

[22] *See* Brad Bushman and Joanne Cantor, *Media Ratings for Violence and Sex: Implications for Policymakers and Parents*, 58, No. 2 AMER. PSYCHOLOGIST 130, 134 (Feb. 2003).

Chapter 5

INTELLECTUAL PROPERTY

The entertainment industry depends on the law of intellectual property to shield its ideas, copyrights, trademarks, trade secrets and patents from theft. This chapter focuses on the legal protection of ideas and fully realized products like films, albums, books, games, and television shows. Talent may capitalize on their intellectual property rights in a myriad of ways.

The Law of Ideas protects story snippets that become the source of films and television shows. Copyright law protects the expression of these ideas, as in a fully realized motion picture version of *Romeo and Juliet*, not just the idea of presenting a version of Shakespeare's play on the silver screen.

Trademarks are symbols or words that are used to designate a particular product, such as "R-Restricted." The Motion Picture Association of America (MPAA) uses this trademark to rate movies for the general public. Even the name of a film or television show may be trademarked if it is going to be applied to merchandise and sold in the marketplace. Some action films, such as in the marketplace. Some action films, such as *Batman*, may ultimately generate more revenue from selling merchandise than movie tickets.

Patent protection was used initially in the entertainment industry to protect camera, film, music, and television equipment and other innovations in merchandizing. Companies obtain patents on the machines they create to display or perform the entertainment products. The general requirements to obtain a patent will be discussed below along with some of the more famous patents that enabled the United States entertainment industry to metamorphose into a global enterprise.

This chapter discusses the various components of intellectual property law and how they apply to the entertainment business.

A. THE LAW OF IDEAS

Ideas are the livelihood of the entertainment industry, because the difference between one star-crossed lover story and another can be millions of dollars. In the film industry, for example, ideas are either pitched orally or submitted in a written treatment, which is a short summary of the story, its plotlines, and any other important details.

Ideas are often presented as an intersection between two well-known films, such as *"Star Wars* meets *Romeo and Juliet"* or *"The Graduate* meets *Lord of the Rings."* One producer pitched former NBC executive Brandon Tartikoff the idea of "Noah's Ark: the Miniseries," or "*Roots* with animals." Tartikoff, *supra* note 6, at 19. Such shorthand gives the studio executive a sense of what the final product might look like.

Similarly, books and television shows may be presented as an idea. Authors often send agents and publishers a book proposal, which includes a one to two-page summary of their fictional or non-fictional manuscript along with author background information, a statement of competitors, and an indication of where the book fits in the marketplace.

A writer, director, producer, show runner, or an ordinary person may present a television show idea to a studio executive with connections in the industry. Due to the limits to the 12-tone scale, it is rarer to pitch a music idea and cases charging theft of musical ideas are uncommon compared to those filed in the other components of the entertainment industry. Plaintiffs are more likely to sue for violation of the copyright to the entire musical work, which will be discussed later in this chapter

Legally, the Law of Ideas falls in the middle between no protection and full protection afforded by copyright, trademark, and patent law. The Law of Ideas restricts the free use of ideas by others and delays the benefit to society of having complementary access to the idea. It grants the creator the right to obtain compensation from those who benefit when he or she discloses an idea to another in confidence. The purpose of the compensation is to reward the creator.

While this may seem straightforward, that those who generate ideas should be compensated for them, there can be a long road between the moment of disclosing the idea and the receipt of compensation. In *Desny v. Wilder*, 46 Cal. 2d 715, 299 P.2d 257 (Cal. Sup. Ct. 1956), the court spoke of ideas as being "free as the air and as speech and senses, and as potent or weak, interesting or drab." Nevertheless, it observed, "there can be circumstances when neither air nor ideas may be acquired without cost."

Ideas may be protected by either express or implied contracts. With an express contract, the parties state in words the terms under which one will compensate the other for the disclosure and use of the idea. With an implied contract, it is the parties conduct that indicates the contract exists. It thus becomes a question of fact as to whether the parties agreed that one would compensate the other for the use of an idea that was confidentially disclosed. Courts are left to decipher whether the parties intended to create a contract by either words or deeds.

In *Blaustein v. Burton*, 9 Cal. App. 3d 161, 88 Cal. Rptr. 319 (Cal. App. 1970), the California Court of Appeals declared there were sufficient facts to imply that the defendants—

Richard Burton, Elizabeth Taylor Burton and Franco Zeffirelli—had agreed to compensate the plaintiff Julian Blaustein for the use of his ideas. The court found that Blaustein disclosed the following ideas to the Burtons, their agent, and to Franco Zeffirelli:

(a) to produce a film based on William Shakespeare's *The Taming of the Shrew*;

(b) to cast Richard Burton and Elizabeth Taylor Burton as the stars;

(c) to have Franco Zeffirelli, a stage director unknown in the United States who at that time had never directed a motion picture, direct the film;

(d) to eliminate the so-called "frame" (i.e., the play within a play device which Shakespeare employed), and begin the film with the main body of the story;

(e) to include in the film version the two key scenes (i.e., the wedding scene and the wedding night scene) which in Shakespeare's play occur offstage and are merely described by a character on stage;

(f) to film the picture in Italy, in the actual Italian settings described by Shakespeare.

The court found that all these ideas were eventually incorporated into the film *The Taming of the Shrew*, which starred Elizabeth Taylor and Richard Burton, was directed by Franco Zeffirelli, and was filmed in Italy. The court reversed the grant of summary judgment to the defendants, holding that there was sufficient evidence to raise a triable issue of fact as to whether there was an implied contract to compensate Blaustein at the going rate of a producer for the use of his ideas.

The most difficult idea to protect is one based on copyrighted fictional characters. Timothy Burton Anderson wrote a thirty-one page treatment entitled "Rocky IV" after seeing the film *Rocky III*. Anderson met with a member of the MGM board of directors and MGM's president to discuss his treatment, which incorporated characters created by Sylvester Stallone and named Stallone as co-author. At the meeting, the MGM people had Anderson sign a release form, relieving MGM from liability for the use of the treatment, but supposedly promising him "big bucks" if they used his treatment.

After *Rocky IV* was made into a feature film, Anderson saw a screening and sued. In *Anderson v. Stallone*, 1989 WL 206431 (C.D. Cal. 1989), a United States District Court declared Anderson's treatment to be an infringing work not entitled to copyright protection. The court found Stallone's characters to be so highly delineated that they warranted copyright protection. Anderson had in essence created nothing of real value.

Individuals like Anderson who develop ideas in the entertainment industry must be careful about the conditions under which they disclose an idea. If the person blurts the idea out, he or she may lose all rights to the idea. To establish the conditions to create an implied contract, there must be some semblance of confidentiality in the relationship and as Anderson found out, the individual must have something worthy of protection. Even that may not be enough.

Anderson had signed a release agreement with MGM, which is a common practice in the entertainment industry as Hollywood production companies seek to protect themselves from charges of idea theft. Barry Spinello signed a similar release agreement to get Steven Speilberg's then production company, Amblin Entertainment, to look at his script, "Adrien and the Toy People." Amblin rejected Spinello's script by a letter dated April 24, 1990. In April 1992, *Daily Variety* announced that Amblin had purchased "Small Soldiers" from Gavin Scott, a British screenwriter.

Based solely on the *Daily Variety* article, Spinello concluded that "Small Soldiers" was based on his "Adrien and the Toy People" and sued. In *Spinello v. Amblin Entertainment*, 34 Cal. Rptr. 2d 695 (Cal. App. Ct. 1994), the court addressed the question of whether the release agreement, which required arbitration in the event of a dispute, was a contract of adhesion. The court concluded that it was not because "Spinello had the opportunity to negotiate and simply failed to do so." *Id.* at 1397. The court then found that the agreement was "patently fair to all parties" and remanded with directions to the trial court to compel arbitration. *Id.* at 1399.

For several decades up until the year 2000, New York state law required a property interest in an idea to make it protectible. To obtain that property interest, the idea must be novel, original, and unique. This concept was illustrated in *Murray v. NBC*, 844 F.2d 933 (2nd Cir. 1988), when Hwesu Murray sued NBC, claiming that it stole his idea for "Father's Day" when it created *The Cosby Show*. The Second Circuit held that Murray's ideal lacked novelty and originality as Bill Cosby himself had discussed the idea of creating a Black television family in non-stereotypical roles. While the court acknowledged that this was a breakthrough, it was represented by the achievement of many Black Americans, including Bill Cosby himself. *Id.*

In *Nadel v. Play-By-Play Toys & Novelties, Inc.*, 208 F.3d 368 (2d Cir. 2000), the Second Circuit held that New York law had abrogated *Murray v. NBC* by adopting a "novelty to the buyer" standard when it comes to protecting ideas by contract law. The court stated, "While an idea may be unoriginal or non-novel in a general sense, it may have substantial value to a particular buyer who is unaware of it and therefore willing to enter into a contract to acquire and exploit it." *Id.* at 377. The novelty to the buyer is much easier to prove than general novelty and originality, although the *Nadel* court was careful to point out that there may be some ideas that are "so unoriginal or lacking in novelty that its obviousness bespeaks widespread and public knowledge of the idea, and such knowledge is therefore imputed to the buyer." *Id.* at 378   The *Nadel* court concluded that a finding of novelty provides sufficient consideration to support contract claims.

The idea case that received the most notoriety was submitted by columnist Art Buchwald in the form of an eight-page treatment to Paramount Pictures. At the time, Paramount was seeking projects for Eddie Murphy. In early 1982, Buchwald, prepared the treatment called "It's a Crude, Crude World" after observing a state visit by the Shah of Iran. He acknowledged that the title was inspired by "It's a Mad, Mad World."

Later in 1982, the eight-page treatment was reduced to three pages and the title was changed to "King for a Day."   In 1983, Paramount registered the title with the Motion Picture Association of America (MPAA). On March 22, 1983, the two parties entered into an agreement to have Paramount purchase the rights to Buchwald's story and concept. At the later trial, a Paramount executive testified that in his ten years at the company, they had never optioned a treatment, though they frequently optioned screenplays. *See* Buchwald v. Paramount Pictures, 13 U.S.P.Q.2d (BNA) 1497 (Cal. Superior Ct. 1990).

In Sept./Oct. 1983, Paramount extended the option by paying Buchwald $2500. On Oct. 16, 1984, Paramount paid Buchwald an additional $10,000 to extend the option for a third time. The contract specified that if Paramount produced a feature length theatrical motion picture based upon Buchwald's treatment, it would pay him a percentage of net profits.

Paramount hired Tad Murphy to write the screenplay, but it did not like his first draft. It then hired French writer and director, Francis Veber to draft another screenplay and paid him $300,000. On March 29, 1985, Paramount decided to abandon "King for a Day" after having invested in excess of $418,000 in developing it. Buchwald optioned his "King for a Day" treatment to Warner Brothers in May 1986. It cancelled the project in January 1988 after discovering that Paramount was shooting *Coming to America* with Eddie Murphy.

Because Buchwald had an express contract with Paramount, he was in a superior position to sue Paramount than those plaintiffs who try to establish the existence of a quasi contract based on oral agreements. For Buchwald, his case turned on whether Paramount had breached his contract by basing *Coming to America* on "King for a Day" and not compensating him. The court ruled that it had in the first phrase of the trial. The next two phases of the trial, which addressed the nature of Buchwald's compensation, will be discussed

later   in   Chapter   7   on   Credits   and
Compensation.

B. COPYRIGHT

Congress is empowered under Article 1,
Section 8, Clause 8 of the U.S. Constitution, "to
Promote the Progress of Science and useful
Arts, by securing for limited Times to Authors
and Inventors the exclusive Right to their
respective Writings and Discoveries." Congress
first implemented this provision with the
Copyright Act of 1790, which was modeled on
England's Statute of Anne, 8 Anne, c.19 (1709).
By implementing the first copyright law,
England produced a breakthrough against
piracy that arose after the invention of the first
printing press in 1450 by German Johannes
Gutenberg and the second 26 years later by
Englishman William Claxton.

Prior to the invention of these printing
presses, monks and scribners copied books by
hand, averaging a book a year. With this slow
process of producing books, authors worried
little about others stealing their work. Indeed,
the book that was reproduced most often was
The Bible. The printing press revolutionized the
manufacture of books, permitting mass
reproduction and theft of original works.

The Statute of Anne protected authors'
works for 14 years, after which it fell into the
public domain. The U.S. Copyright Act of 1790
gave authors an initial 14 years of protection

with the option to renew for an additional 14 years. Since that time, the duration of copyright has been extended numerous times to the current lifetime of the individual author/entertainer plus 70 years. In the case of joint owners, the copyright expires 70 years after the death of the last surviving author. Corporate, anonymous, pseudonymous, and work for hire authors enjoy protection for a flat 95 years.

While Congress initially protected only books, charts, and maps, it has expanded coverage of new forms of art and technology as they have been invented. Congress began protecting photographs in 1865, motion pictures in 1912, sound recordings in 1972, and computer disks in 1976.

1. COPYRIGHT REQUIREMENTS

There are three requirements for an item to be copyrightable. It must possess all the following:

1. Copyrightable subject matter
2. Fixation in a tangible medium of expression
3. Originated with or created by the author

Books, motion pictures, television shows, music, theatrical plays and choreographic notes are copyrightable subject matter under the statute as they are obviously fixed in a tangible medium of expression. They are physical and can be touched and handled. Theaters show movies from reels and buyers can purchase them in DVD or VHS formats. Television shows are also played from tapes or digital format in studios, or downloaded from a satellite feed. Music can be physically rendered in sheet music, on tapes, or CDs.

The necessity that a work originate with the author produces some disputes particularly when an allegation of plagiarism surfaces. In bringing an action for theft, the plaintiff maintains that the defendant's work originated with the plaintiff. Originality can have a dual meaning when it comes to derivative works. The courts also ask whether the newcomer contributed anything new or novel to the first work.

In *Gracen v. Bradford Exchange*, 698 F.2d 300 (7th Cir. 1983), Jorie Gracen won a competition to paint figures from the MGM film *The Wizzard of Oz*. When she didn't like the contract, she refused to sign it and later sued after Bradford Exchange copied her painting. The court ruled that her painting, derived from the MGM movie stills, was not sufficiently original to warrant copyright protection. Because Gracen produced a derivative work, the court seemed to impose a higher originality standard, requiring substantial differences between the original and the derivative to make the latter copyrightable.

2. COPYRIGHT FORMALITIES

Copyright formalities include providing a notice that ownership is claimed in the work and registering the work with the Copyright Office, which is housed in the basement of the Library of Congress in Washington, D.C. To give notice to the world that an author claims copyright to a given item, he or she must include the following information on the work:

Copyright or ©, name and year.

In books, this information is normally printed on the first inside page, known as the copyright page. For movies and television shows, the copyright credit is usually the last to be shown on the screen. For music, notice is written on the CD in the form of the letter p in a circle (p) to indicate that a performance copyright is claimed. Visual artists may place the notice on the back of the painting or on the bottom of a sculpture because they do not want to ruin the artistic presentation of their work. This notice form alerts the world that copyright protection is claimed in the book.

Up until 1989, the United States required that notice be placed on the work by the author or the work fell into the public domain, which permitted anyone to use the work without compensating the author. The author had a five-year period to cure the problem by republishing with notice. During this time, notice was completely optional in most other countries in the world.

After Congress passed the Berne Implementation Act amendments to the Copyright Law, which became effective on March 1, 1989, copyright notice became optional. Works are automatically protected whether or not the authors places a notice on them. The U.S. law continues to provide incentives to encourage citizens to apply notice to their works. By applying a notice to the work, the copyright holder eliminates the innocent infringer defense, whereby someone claims they did not know that the work was subject to copyright protection. Notice makes it clear that copyright law covers the work.

Another copyright formality is to register the work with the U.S. Copyright Office. To do so, the author must fill out the copyright forms, pay the applicable fee, and deposit two copies of the best edition of the work. The forms to register the work can be found at www.loc.gov/copyright.

The forms are set up by category. Form TX is used to register books, brochures, computer programs, games, poetry, and speeches. Form PA is the appropriate one for television shows, motion pictures, including screenplays and musical works that accompany motion pictures. Form SR is employed for all "fixation of a series of musical, spoken, or other sounds, but not including the sounds accompanying a motion picture or other audiovisual work."

While registering the work is also optional, it remains a prerequisite before U.S. nationals can initiate a suit in U.S. courts. Under the Digital Millennium Copyright Act signed into law by President Clinton on October 28, 1998, foreign works are exempt from this requirement.

Registration does, however, provide prima facie evidence that the author owns the work. Depositing two copies of the best edition of the work (i.e. two DVDs or VHS copies) is also no longer a prerequisite to suit, but fines may be imposed if the Library of Congress requests the work and the author declines to send it. The fines are often the equivalent of what it would cost the Library of Congress to purchase two copies of the work.

3. COPYRIGHT OWNERSHIP AND TRANSFER

In most instances, the person who actually creates the work is considered the owner of the copyright. Nevertheless, film, television, music, games, theater and dance, and jointly authored books are collaborative processes with two or more creative people contributing to the final output. On any given film, for example, the following supply their talent: writers, actors, directors, producers, set designers, wardrobe designers, make-up artists, camera operators, editors, soundtrack composers, stunt performers, special effects supervisors, animators, and lighting designers. Music may be produced with the assistance of sound engineers and producers.

Without copyright ownership defined by contracts, customs and statutes, anyone who contributed to the final output of an entertainment product could claim authorship of the film and inhibit its exploitation. The work for hire doctrine resolves problems concerning authorship and copyright ownership.

Section 101 of the U.S. copyright statute defines a work made for hire as:

(1) a work prepared by an employee within the scope of his or her employment; or
(2) a work specially ordered or commissioned for use as a contribution to a collective work, as a part of a motion picture or other audiovisual work, as a translation, as a supplementary work, as a compilation, as an instructional text, as a test, as answer material for a test, or as an atlas, if the parties expressly agree in a written instrument signed by them that the work shall be considered a work made for hire.

In the film industry, for example, contributions to motion pictures fall under subsection 2. Although screenwriters, for example, will be given credit for writing the film and can copyright the script individually, once they sell the script, their work becomes incorporated into the film and is considered a work made for hire. The studio or production company will copyright the film in its corporate name.

While no written instrument is required in the case of an employee work, a written instrument is required in the case of a work prepared on special order or commission to make it a "work made for hire."

This requirement of a writing for specially ordered works under subsection (2) means that the creator of that type of work must consciously--assuming the contract is read--give up the copyright to the work that he or she would normally possess. By contrast, with employee works produced within the scope of employment under subsection (1), the act presumes the employer to be the author and requires an express written instrument signed by both parties for the employee to retain any of the rights comprised in the copyright.

Another form of collaboration is to work jointly with another author. The copyright statute defines a "joint work" as a work prepared by two or more authors with the intention that their contributions be merged into inseparable or interdependent parts of a unitary whole. The confusion arises when others feel their collaboration is worthy of author credit. The question then centers on the nature of their contributions and the intent of the parties.

In *Aalmuhammed v. Lee*, 202 F.3d 1227, 1233 (9 th Cir. 2000), the court noted that in film, "Everyone from the producer and director to casting director, costumer, hairstylist, and 'best boy' gets listed in the movie credits because all of their creative contributions really do matter." Nevertheless, they are not all entitled to proclaim themselves as authors or coauthors of the film. In this instance, the court declared that "neither Aalmuhammed, nor Spike Lee, nor Warner Brothers, made any objective manifestations of an intent to be coauthors.... Aalmuhammed offered no evidence that he was the 'inventive or master mind' of the movie." *Id.* at 1235.

4. MORAL RIGHTS & COLORIZATION

The concept of moral rights originated in France where they are known as *droit moral* and include the following:

1. *Right to Create*, which prohibits the completion of a work from being judicially mandated;

2. *Right of Disclosure*, which permits the author to determine when to make the work public;

3. *Right to Withdraw Work* after it has been disclosed, which is a limited right that applies only to publishing houses and requires the author to indemnify the publisher for losses;

4. *Right of Name Attribution (or Authorship)*, which entitles the author (a) to be recognized as the creator of the work, (b) to anonymously or pseudonymously publish the work, (c) to prevent the work from being attributed to another, and (d) to stop his or her name from being used on works that he or she did not create or that later became distorted;

5. *Right of Integrity*, which allows the author to prevent alterations, distortions or destruction of his work; and

6. *Right of Protection from Excessive Criticism*, which permits the author to publish a reply to unjustified criticism.

The United States officially recognizes the Right of Authorship and the Right of Integrity in 17 U.S.C. §106A, but only gives these rights to visual artists. See, e.g., Sherri Burr, *Introducing Art Law*, 37 COPYRIGHT WORLD 22, 24 (Feb. 1994). The entertainment industry has looked to other aspects of U.S. law for protection.

For example the "Right to Create" can be found in the prohibition against specifically enforcing personal service contracts. The Right of Disclosure relates to the Copyright Act's grant of the right to copy under 17 U.S.C. § 106. Entertainers who seek "The Right of Protection from Excessive Criticism" may find it in U.S. libel law. As for protection against distortions, sometimes entertainers have found relief under 15 U.S.C. § 1125 of the Lanham Act, which prohibits false designation of origin and false description.

In *Gilliam v. ABC*, for example, the British writers and performers known as Monty Python sued ABC to restrain the network from broadcasting edited versions of three separate programs that allegedly violated the Lanham Act. 538 F.2d 14, 24 (2nd Cir. 1976). Monty Python argued that the cuts for commercials and U.S. censorship standards amounted to a mutilation or misrepresentation of their work. The court found that the Lanham Act could be used "to prevent misrepresentations that injure plaintiff's business or personal reputation." *Id.* The court quoted another case to augment its point that "[t]o deform his work is to present him to the public as the creator of a work not his own, and thus makes him subject to criticism for work he has not done." *Id.* The court directed the district court to issue a preliminary injunction against ABC.

The *Gilliam* case is an example of how the moral rights principal of the "Right of Integrity" can be found in other aspects of U.S. laws, which protect entertainers from having others distort their work. ABC had omitted 24 of the original 90 minutes of script, leaving segments that were disjointed and difficult to follow. In one segment, the court noted, "[t]he ABC edit eliminates [the] middle sequence so that the father is comfortably dressed at one moment and, in the next moment, is shown in a soaked condition without any explanation for the change in his appearance. *Id.* at 25.

Moreover, due to the global nature of the entertainment industry, some U.S. citizens have sought moral rights relief in France. In *Turner Entertainment v. Huston*, 16 Ent. L. Rptr. 10:3 (1995), the children of the director John Huston sued Turner Entertainment for colorizing Huston's work *Asphalt Jungle*. Huston's heirs argued that it was a violation of his moral rights to add color to a film that Huston had deliberately chosen to film in black and white to create the right atmosphere. Huston said about another one of his black and white films, *The Maltese Falcon*, "I wanted to shoot it in black and white like a sculptor to work in clay, to pour his work in bronze, to sculpt in marble."

Turner Entertainment fought for the right to colorize the film, claiming that as the copyright holder, it was "the author" of the film. The French court separated the economic rights in the film, which were held by Turner Entertainment, from the moral rights, which were held by Huston, and enjoined the showing of the film on French television. The court also ordered Turner Entertainment to pay 200,000 French francs in damages and costs.

5. COPYRIGHT INFRINGEMENT & REMEDIES

The copyright holder is entitled to the following exclusive rights under Section 106 of the U.S. Copyright Act, subject to the limitations found in section 107 through 121:

(1) to reproduce the copyrighted work in copies or phonorecords

(2) to prepare derivative works based on the copyrighted work;

(3) to distribute copies or phonorecords of the copyrighted work to the public by sale or other transfer of ownership, or by rental, lease or lending;

(4) in the case of literary, musical, dramatic, and choreographic works, pantomimes, and motion pictures and other audiovisual works, to perform the copyrighted work publicly;

(5) in the case of literary, musical, dramatic, and choreographic works, pantomimes, and pictorial, graphic, or sculptural works, including the individual images of a motion picture or other audiovisual work, to display the copyrighted work publicly; and

(6) in the case of sound recordings, to perform the copyrighted work publicly by means of a digital audio transmission.

17 U.S.C. § 106. Further, section 501(a) provides, "Anyone who violates any of the exclusive rights of the copyright owner . . . is an infringer of the copyright or right of the author, as the case may be." 17 U.S.C. § 501.

To prove copyright infringement, the plaintiff must establish (1) that he or she owns the copyrighted work; and (2) that the defendant copied the work or took another exclusive right of the plaintiff. To determine whether a defendant has infringed a plaintiff's copyright, courts use words such as theft or plagiarism to refer to the unauthorized taking of one party's work by another. The plaintiff may offer either direct or circumstantial evidence to prove the unauthorized taking. Circumstantial evidence consists of showing that the defendant had access to the copyrighted work and that there exists a substantial similarity of ideas and expression between the plaintiff's and defendant's works.

In copyright infringement cases, courts primarily analyze facts. It is crucial to track the major and some of the minor similarities between the two works and compare them to public domain works. To succeed, a plaintiff must show that the defendant could only have produced his work by copying the plaintiff's work.

The following subsections explore how copyright infringement cases relate to film, television, music, publishing, and interactive games.

a. Film Infringement

With film infringement cases, the original copyright holder may be the author of a book, a screenplay, a play, a treatment, or even another film. The question becomes whether the defendant's work came from the plaintiff's copyrighted piece or a public domain source, such as an expired copyrighted work or factual material.

In *Sheldon v. MGM Pictures*, 81 F.2d 49 (2nd Cir. 1936, *cert denied* 298 U.S. 669 (1936), the court considered whether the movie *Letty Lynton* starring Joan Crawford came from the book by the same name or the defendant's play. Both the book and the play were based on a true story of a Scottish girl name Madeleine Smith who was tried for attempting to and actually poisoning her French lover, Emile L'Angelier, after he threatened to reveal their relationship to her new fiancé. L'Angelier died after drinking arsenic-laced hot chocolate. Smith was acquitted when her sister testified that on one of the poisoning occasions, they had slept together in a bed throughout the night. On the other alleged poisoning occasion, Smith's fiancé swore that she had been with him at the theater.

The court found the defendants' film *Letty Lynton* to be substantially similar to the plaintiff's play named "Madeleine Cary," which the defendants initially sought to purchase and turn into a movie. When the head of an association of motion pictures thought the play obscene, MGM purchased instead the movie rights to the book *Letty Lynton.*

The court said, "The defendants took for their *mis en scène* the same city and the same social class; and they chose a South American villain." *Id.* at 54. The court also noted that Letty Lynton "tracked" Madeleine Cary in her passion at the beginning, her errant parent, the death scenes and the district attorney investigation at the end. Both lovers use Gaucho songs to woo the heroines and both die of strychnine not arsenic as in the original story and the book. The court concludes, "[I]f the picture was not an infringement of the play, there can be none short of taking the dialogue." *Id.* at 56,

Other film cases have questioned whether commercials infringed a film, and whether film advertising was stolen from magazine covers. In *MGM v. American Honda Motor Co.*, 900 F. Supp. 1287 (C.D. Cal. 1995), MGM claimed that Honda violated their copyrights to sixteen James Bond films and infringed their rights to the James Bond character through their commercial for the Honda del Sol automobile. The court ruled in MGM's favor finding that film scenes and characters were copyrightable.

In *Steinberg v. Columbia Pictures*, 663 F.Supp. 706 (S.D.N.Y. 1987), Saul Steinberg claimed that Columbia Pictures violated the copyright in his illustration for the March 29, 1976 issue of *The New Yorker* magazine that Columbia Pictures used to advertise its film *Moscow on the Hudson* starring Robin Williams. In ruling for Steinberg, the court found the Columbia Pictures' poster substantially similar to Steinberg's because it symbolized the same myopic view of the world, used the same typeface, spiky lettering and whimsical, sketchy style as the plaintiff's illustration. *Id.* at 710.

Nevertheless, when Paramount Pictures Corp was inspired by Annie Leibovitz's *Vanity Fair* cover of a pregnant Demi Moore to create a movie poster with actor Leslie Nielsen's face attached to a pregnant body, the court in *Leibovitz v. Paramount Pictures*, 137 F.3d 109 (2d Cir. 1998), determined that was not infringement. Rather, it found it an acceptable parody under the fair use doctrine, which will be discussed in more detail later in this chapter.

b. Television Infringement

The challenges to television infringement determine whether a defendant has taken a particular type of television show. In *Sid & Mary Crofft Television Productions v. McDonalds's Corp..* 562 F.2d 1157 (9th Cir. 1977), the plaintiffs charged that the defendants infringed their "H. R. Pufnstuf" children's television show by the production of their "McDonaldland" television commercials. The district court found that the defendants had infringed and the court of appeals affirmed that decision, finding that there was sufficient proof of infringement.

The Los Angeles News Service (LANS) sued Reuters Television for rebroadcasting its copyrighted video and audio tape recording of the Reginald Denny beating during the April 1992 riots. *See* Los Angeles News Service v. Reuters Television, 149 F.3d 987 (9th Cir. 1998).

LANS licensed the work to NBC to be used on the *Today* show. A group of Reuters defendants and their partner Visnews International simultaneously retransmitted the *Today* show to Europe and Africa by satellite. While the Court of Appeals noted that the Copyright Act does not apply extraterritorially, it does apply to initial infringing acts that take place in New York. The Court of Appeals considered the satellite transmissions to be "merely a means of shipping the unlicensed footage abroad for further dissemination." *Id.* at 991. The Court of Appeals held that LANS could recover damages "flowing from exploitation abroad of the domestic acts of infringement committed by defendants." *Id.* at 992.

c. Music Infringement

During the Mozart's era,[23] composers constantly took other musicians' themes and composed variations. In the movie *Amadeus*, Mozart tells Salieri upon their first meeting that he once composed variations on one of Salieri's themes.

Salieri bows and says, "You do me great honor."

---

[23] This write-up of this incident initially appeared in Sherri L. Burr, *The Piracy Gap: Protecting Intellectual Property in an Era of Artistic Creative and Technological Change*, 33:1 WILLAMETTE L. REV. 245, 247 (Winter 1997). It is reprinted with permission.

Mozart responds, "Funny little theme but it yielded some great results."

Salieri grimaces.

This exchange illustrates that during that time, imitation was considered a means of flattery, and not of theft. Eventually, that attitude would change as more and more musicians associated copyright protection with their ability to earn a living.

There have been several famous music infringement cases from the 1947 *Arnstein v. Porter*, to the 2001 *A & M Records v. Napster.* Along the way, George Harrison was sued in the 1970s for lifting "He's So Fine" from The Chiffons to create his "My Sweet Lord." In the 1980s, Vanilla Ice was alleged to have stolen a song from the British group Queen to make his hit "Ice, Ice Baby," and Biz Markie was accused of sampling or incorporating three words from Gilbert O' Sullivan's "Alone Again (Naturally)" in his "Alone Again."

In Biz Markie's case, the first sentence of Judge Duffy's opinion cited *The Bible*'s seventh commandment, "Thou shalt not steal." Grand Upright Music Ltd. v. Warner Bros. Records, Inc., 780 F.Supp. 182, 183 (S.D.N.Y.1991). The court expressed concern that "the defendants in this action for copyright infringement would have this court believe that stealing is rampant in the music business and, for that reason, their conduct here should be excused."

However, the court noted that Biz Markie's conduct violated "not only the Seventh Commandment, but also the copyright laws of this country." *Id.* Because Biz Markie and his collaborators had their attorney contact the brother/agent of O'Sullivan in search of consent, the judged deemed this as evidence that the "defendants knew they were violating the plaintiff's rights." *Id.* at 185.

Ira Arnstein claimed Cole Porter stole several of his compositions, some of which had been had already been made public, but others of which were private. The court acknowledged that some of Arnstein's claims seemed "fantastic," such as his allegation that Porter "had stooges right along to follow me, watch me, and live in the same apartment with me." 154 F.2d 464, 467 (2nd Cir. 1947). Nevertheless, the court felt that Arnstein's credibility should be left up to the jury.

The *Arnstein* court established the Lay Audience test: "whether defendant took from plaintiff's work so much of what is pleasing to the ears of lay listeners who comprise the audience for such popular music is composed, that defendant wrongfully appropriated something which belongs to the plaintiff." *Id.* at 473. The court felt that this was "an issue of fact which a jury is peculiarly fitted to determine." *Id.* The court reversed a grant of summary judgment and remanded the case for a jury trial.

Judge Tang, writing for the Ninth Circuit, followed similar logic in his opinion reversing summary judgment for MCA and remanding the question of whether the theme from the motion picture *ET: The Extra-Terrestrial* came from Les Baxter's copyrighted song "Joy." Baxter v. MCA, 812 F.2d 421 (9th Cir. 1987). Baxter claimed that Academy Award-winning composer John Williams was familiar with his work, having played "Joy" in the Hollywood Bowl in the 1960s before creating "Theme from E.T." in the 1980s.

MCA attached the following items to their motion for summary judgment: (1) cassette tape recordings of "Joy" as it appeared on the album "The Passions" and the movie soundscore of "Theme from E.T.": (2) the twenty-three page written instrumental sheet music of "Joy" that was copyrighted; and (3) the five-page piano score of the "Theme from E.T." Baxter introduced expert testimony and five comparison tapes by Professor Harvey Bacal regarding the degree of similarity between the two works.

In granting summary judgment for Williams and MCA, the district court judge wrote,

> This court's 'ear' is as lay as they come. The Court cannot hear any substantial similarity between defendant's expression of the idea and plaintiff's. Until Professor Bacal's tapes were listened to, the Court could not even tell what the complaint was about. Granted that Professor Bacal's comparison exposes a

musical similarity in sequence of notes which would, perhaps, be obvious to experts, the similarity of expression (or impression as a whole) is totally lacking and could not be submitted to a jury.

Id. at 423.

The Court of Appeals reversed, holding "[W]e cannot say that "Joy" and "Theme from E.T." are so dissimilar that reasonable minds could not differ as to a lack of substantial similarity between them." The court was careful to reject defendants' contention that "any similarity between the works can be reduced to a six-note sequence which is not protectible under the copyright laws."

Another important issue is whether providing musical equipment can lead to charges of contributory infringement. The standard for contributory infringement is that the secondary infringer "know or have reason to know" of direct infringement. *A & M Records v. Napster*, 239 F.3d 1004, 1020 (9th Cir. 2001) (citations omitted).

On December 6, 1999, A & M Records and seventeen other record companies filed a complaint for contributory and vicarious copyright infringement and sought an injunction against Napster, Inc., an Internet start-up company. *A & M Records, Inc. v. Napster*, 114 F.Supp.2d 896, 900 (N.D. Cal. 2000). The district court enjoined Napster from "engaging in, or facilitating others in copying, downloading, uploading, transmitting, or distributing plaintiffs' copyrighted musical compositions and sound recordings, protected either by federal or state law, with express permission of the rights owners." *Id.* at 927.

While Napster did not directly copy music from other computers, the Ninth Circuit Court of Appeals found that it had designed and operated a system that permitted "the transmission and retention of sound recordings employing digital technology." A & M Records v. Napster, 239 F.3d 1004, 1011 (9th Cir. 2001). The court noted the district court's determination that as much as "eighty-seven percent of the files available on Napster may be copyrighted and more than seventy percent may be owned or administered by plaintiffs." Napster did not challenge the district court's conclusion that the plaintiffs could establish Napster's liability as a contributory infringer. The court of appeals agreed that Napster had knowledge, both actual and constructive, of direct infringement, and materially contributed to the infringing activity by providing "the site and facilities" for direct infringement." *Id.* at 1020-1022.

d. Publishing Infringement

Book authors and freelance writers have also sued or been sued for copyright infringement. In *Hoehling v. Universal City Studios*, A.A. Hoehling claimed that another author and a movie company lifted his theory that the Hindenburg was sabotaged by Eric Spehl to please his lady friend. Michael McDonald Mooney, another author, consulted Hoehling's book *Who Destroyed the Hindenburg* while writing his literary version of the Hindenburg disaster called *The Hindenburg.* 618 F.2d. 972 (2nd Cir. 1980). Mooney sold the movie rights to his book to Universal Studios. The court said that notwithstanding Hoehling's valid copyright in his work, he could not protect his historical interpretation of facts or a number of specific facts, as these were not copyrightable as a matter of law. *Id.*

In *New York Times v. Tasini,* 533 U.S. 483 (2001), six freelance authors sued the *New York Times* for copyright infringement for placing their articles on its computer database without their consent. The freelance authors charged that their contracts with the *Times* did not include the right to place their articles in an electronic database.

The publishers claimed that they could republish the articles on their database under 17 U.S.C. § 201 (c), which provides

"Copyright in each separate contribution to a collective work is distinct from copyright in the collective work as a whole, and vests initially in the author of the contribution. In the absence of an express transfer of the copyright or of any rights under it, the owner of copyright in the collective work is

> presumed to have acquired only the privilege of reproducing and distributing the contribution as part of that particular collective work, any revision of that collective work, and any later collective work in the same series."

The publishers maintained that section 201 accorded them as copyright owners of collective works a privilege to reproduce and distribute the authors' works. *Id.* at 488. The Supreme Court disagreed, holding that the publishers infringed the author's copyrights by reproducing and distributing the articles in a manner not authorized by the authors and not privileged by § 201 (c).

In *Feist Publications v. Rural Telephone Service Co.*, 499 U.S. 340 (1990), the Supreme Court considered whether phone books were copyrightable in light of the fact/expression dichotomy that affects writers of nonfiction works. As similarly discussed in *Hoehling,* because facts are not original to a particular author, they cannot be copyrighted.

The Supreme Court noted that while the copyright statute does not protect facts, it does protect compilations, if the author demonstrates originality. In a prior court decision, the court established that "originality requires independent creation and a modicum of creativity" and defined "author" as "he to whom anything owes its origin."

The copyright laws protect writings that are the fruit of intellectual labor embodied in the form of books, prints, engravings, and the like. The Court noted that "[S]ince facts do not owe their origin to an act of authorship, they are not original and, thus, are not copyrightable." *Id.* at 1285. Nevertheless, the writer of factual compilations have options to choose:

    A. Which facts to include
    B. In what order to place them
    C. How to arrange the data so that readers use them effectively

Id. at 347. This selection & arrangement entails a minimal degree of creativity. A work can be copyrighted, but some parts not protected. Facts must be clothed with original expression, as copyright protection extends only to those elements that owe their origin to the author. Subsequent compilers of facts may use facts contained in another's work.

Compilations, like phone books, are an expression of facts and thus can be copyrighted. Here, Feist took names, telephone numbers, and towns from the Rural phone book that Rural may have been the first to report. However, these items do not owe their origin to Rural. Therefore, Rural cannot own them.

e. Game Infringement

As interactive games have become a popular form of entertainment, so too have evolved their problems with copyright infringement. In *Lewis Galoob Toys v. Nintendo*, 964 F.2d 965 (9th Cir. 1992), *cert denied* 507 U.S. 985 (1993), the Ninth Circuit addressed whether Game Genie violated Nintendo's copyrights.

Simply summarized, Nintendo of America markets a home video game system called Nintendo Entertainment System. The player inserts a Nintendo cartridge containing a video game to use the system. The player controls one of the game's characters and progress by pressing buttons and manipulating a control pad. Galoob manufactures Game Genie, which the player can use to alter up to three features of a Nintendo game by increasing the lives, the speed, and versatility of the Nintendo characters. Game Genie's altering affects on the Nintendo characters are temporary. *Id.* at 967.

Nintendo charged that Lewis Galoob Toys infringed its §102 (2) rights to prepare derivative works. The Ninth Circuit, however, disagreed, finding that Game Genie was not a derivative work, because its audiovisual display was not fixed. While Game Genie generated a $150 million market, the court concluded,

> "[T]he existence of a market does not, and cannot, determine conclusively whether a work is an infringing derivative work. For example, although there is a market for kaleidoscopes, it does not necessarily follow that kaleidoscopes create unlawful derivative works when pointed at protected

artwork. The same can be said of countless other products that enhance, but do not replace, copyrighted works.... The Game Genie does not physically incorporate a portion of a copyrighted work, nor does it supplant demand for a component of that work."

Id. at 969. In holding that Game Genie was not a derivative work, the Ninth Circuit stated, "The Game Genie is useless by itself, it can only enhance, and cannot duplicate or recast a Nintendo game's output." *Id.*

6. FAIR USE

Once the plaintiff has put forth his prima facie case of copyright infringement, the burden then shifts to the defendant to refute the evidence that he stole the plaintiff's work. The defendant can offer proof of independent creation (he or she created his or her own work), that he only took non-copyrightable items from the plaintiff; or that the use was somehow authorized, such as making a fair use of the plaintiff's work.

Section 107 of the U.S. Copyright act requires courts to balance the following four factors to determine whether a defendant has made a fair use of the plaintiff's work:

(1) the purpose and character of the use, including whether such use is of a

commercial nature or is for nonprofit educational purposes;

(2) the nature of the copyrighted work;

(3) the amount and substantiality of the portion used in relation to the copyrighted work as a whole; and

(4) the effect of the use upon the potential market for or value of the copyrighted work.

The fair use statute seems uncomplicated on its face, yet it has generated considerable litigation. The statute does not tell how to weigh the factors, although courts consider some factors more important than others. Through judicial decisions, the fourth factor has become the most important

Because of the balancing requirement, no one can ever be absolutely certain whether he or she has used a work fairly until the use has been litigated and decided by a court. Unfortunately, what the district court may consider fair, the court of appeals may find it unfair, and then the Supreme Court may ultimately decide it is fair. This split happened when Acuff Rose decided to sue the 2 Live Crew over its rap version of *Pretty Woman*. The Supreme Court held that because it was a parody, it might be considered fair so long as the parodist no more than necessary to conjure up and critique the original.   *See* Campbell v. Acuff-Rose Music, Inc., 510 U.S. 569 (1994).

7. REMEDIES

In 17 U.S.C. §§ 502-513, the remedies are set out for infringement. Section 502 provides that any court may issue "temporary and final injunctions on such terms as it may deem reasonable to prevent or restrain infringement of copyright." The injunction may be served anywhere in the United States and shall be operative throughout the United States. This has been one of the most useful remedies employed in successful infringement cases as it keeps the copyright holder from sustaining further losses due to the defendant's actions.

Section 503 permits a court to impound and disposed of all copies, including "plates, molds, matrices, masters, tapes, film negatives, or any other article" used to produce the infringing article.

Section 504 provides that the copyright owner may receive their damages and any profits that accrued to the infringer. The awarding of both is meant to make it expensive for the infringer as they will not only lose any profits that accrued to them but they must reimburse the copyright owner for injuries that they cause.

Section 504 (c) permits the copyright owner to elect to receive statutory damages instead of proving actual damages. The court can award not less than $750 or more than $30,000, as it considers just. If the infringement was particularly willful, the court may in its discretion award of sum of up to $150,000. This can be valuable where, as in the case of _Marcus v. Rowley_, 695 F.2d 1171 (9th Cir. 1983), the plaintiff suffered only $23 in actual damages but the infringement was particularly egregious when the defendant Rowley copied eleven pages of her twenty-four page cake decorating book directly from the plaintiff and did not give her credit or acknowledge her copyright. The Ninth Circuit remanded for a determination of damages.

Successful copyright holders may also sue under Section 505 to obtain their costs and attorneys fees. Any court has discretion to award these fees.

In some instances, individuals may be held criminally liable under section 506 if they infringe a copyright willfully for purposes of commercial advantage or private financial gain. This section also applies for reproducing and distributing copyrighted works valued at more than $1000. The criminal penalties include fines of not more than $250,000 and imprisonment for not more than five years or both. The infringing copies may also be seized and forfeited under section 509.

C. TRADEMARKS & MERCHANDIZING

Valued at $34 billion in the year 2000, the Disney brand name is considered one of the top twelve most valuable trademarks in the world. A trademark can be a word, design, or combination thereof, used by a manufacturer to identify its goods. Trademarks identify the source of the commercial object, guarantee the constancy of the quality, and advertise the manufacturer and attract customers. Trademarks may also describe the product. For example, consumers expect to see a family film when it sees a movie with the Disney label. For that reason, Disney does not permit its subsidiaries to distribute films that have been rated NC-17.

There are several different types of trademarks. Service marks identify services such as [H & R Block]. Certification marks identify goods or services meeting certain qualifications, such as the Motion Picture Association of America (MPAA) ratings marks. When a picture receives a "R-Restricted" rating, the film has been branded with a certification that the film is not suitable for children 17 and under. A collective mark identifies goods, services or members of a collective organization, such as the MPAA. Its members are derived from the major Hollywood Studio Association. Trade names identify the corporation, such as the Walt Disney Company.

Manufactures provide a notice to indicate that they claim a trademark on the good. If the mark is unregistered at the federal level, the claimant will use a common law trademark such as: TM or SM. SM is use to designate a service mark. If the mark has been federally registered then it will look like one of these: ®, or "Registered U.S. Patent & Trademark Office," or "Reg. U.S. Pat. & TM. Off."

While applying one of these notices to the product is not mandatory, it is necessary to obtain damages and eliminate the innocent infringer defense that someone may claim if they did not know about the trademark.

In terms of value, the Disney brand was valued at $28.04 billion in 2003. That value comes from the number of Disney products and services, from theme parks, to motion pictures and television shows, that are available to the general public to purchase.

1. FILM MERCHANDIZING

Merchandizing the products shown in a film or television program can generate considerable revenue for the film's owner. Producers and advertisers count on the public's interest their fictional characters to sell products based on the character or that the character is seen using in the film.

In a typical James Bond film, for example, the character will drive a fancy new car, wear an exclusive watch, or utilize other merchandise. Producers sell product placements in their films to generate additional revenue to offset costs in their production budget. The 1997 James Bond *Tomorrow Never Dies* reportedly secured $110 million in product placement, promotional and merchandizing deals, roughly the same amount as its domestic box office earnings. PAUL WEILER, ENTERTAINMENT MEDIA AND THE LAW 511 (2d. Ed. 2002).

As CNN reported, "Bond has evolved from a suave, English super spy to a flashy, moving billboard for global advertisers such as BMW, Omega watches, Martini vodka, and even construction machinery manufacturer Caterpillar. All those products are prominently featured in the Bond film, *The World is Not Enough.* The Bond attraction is such that companies have been building entire advertising campaigns around products featured in the movie. BMW has made its Bond car an integral part of its marketing strategy, for instance." See *CNN, From Omega to Caterpillar, companies covet 007's cachet,* (Nov.22,1999), *available at* http://www.cnn.com/SHOWBIZ/Movies/9911/ 22/bond.gadgets/.

2. TELEVISION MERCHANDIZING

Similarly in television, producers sell advertising in the form of product placement. The advertiser pays to have a popular television character drink their brand of color or eat their brand of fast foods. They may also pay for the character to visit a particular resort location. The producer receives revenue that helps offset the production budget that pays the stars' and crew salaries as well as set design and so forth.

A corollary is to create merchandise based on a popular show. Cartoons and comic books, for example, can generate toys, apparel, bedroom furniture and posters for the walls. These items are usually produced under a license agreement.

When Margaret Rey initially licensed her children's book *Curious* George to become 104 television episodes, she retained ancillary rights. *See* Rey v. Lafferty, 990 F.2d 1379 (1st Cir. 1993). In January 1983, she signed an Ancillary Products Agreement (APA) with the Canadian investment firm LHP giving the company the right to license "Curious George" spin-off productions for all tangible goods except, in certain instances, books, films, tapes, records or video productions. In return for the rights, Rey was to receive one-third of the royalties on the licensed products, with a guaranteed minimum annual payment, later increased to 50% with no guaranteed minimum payment. She retained the right to disapprove any product, so long as the right was not unreasonably withheld.

Conflict developed over the contract after Rey disapproved of certain products and the royalty revenue declined. Rey sued the companies responsible for exploiting her ancillary rights. She alleged that the companies had wrongfully withheld royalties on the Houghton Mifflin books and Sony videos. She also contended that LHP could not recover damages from her withholding approval of certain ancillary products. The court of appeals ruled in Rey's favor, finding that she was entitled to royalties that had been wrongly withheld, and to refuse to give approval of licensed ancillary products on reasonable grounds. *Id.*

Rey had a contract with LHP to produce license the use of her characters on merchandise. In certain instances, individuals may use characters without obtaining approval. Cartoonists, for example, have been known to parody the products of manufacturers without their permission.

After Jim Henson Productions created "Spa'am," the high priest of a tribe of wild boars that worship Miss Piggy as Queen Sha Ka La Ka La for the movie *Muppett Treasure Island*, the Hormel Corporation sued. Hormel Foods Corp v. Jim Henson Productions, 73 F.3d 497 (2nd Cir. 1996). Hormel claimed the "Spa'am" character violated its trademark SPAM used for luncheon meat. Hormel expressed concern that "Spa'am" the boar would make consumers worry about the quality of its meat products and that sales of SPAM will drop off if it is linked with "evil in porcine form." *Id.* at 501.

The court however disagreed, finding Henson's Spa'am to be a parody, which distinguished it from Hormel's products. The court did not accept Hormel's arguments that consumers would be confused between merchandise carrying the SPAM logo and products featuring Spa'am the wild boar. *Id.* at 505.

3. MUSIC MERCHANDIZING

Bands tend to sell their merchandise while on tour as fans seek mementos to memorialize the evening. At live music events, be it a rap or rock concerts, bands or their licensed agents sell t-shirts, programs, hats, posters along with the CDs. Even at classical music concerts, fans will have opportunities to at least purchase the CDs.

Some companies license the use of musicians names to apply to concert merchandise in anticipation of a certain number of attendees. Great Entertainment Merchandising (GEM) paid Vince Neil (VN) Merchandizing a $1,000,000 advance against royalties in anticipation of a Vince Neil concert tour before 800,000 paid attendees. The contract was signed with VN Merchandising, a loan out company created the day before to enter into the agreement. It specified that that VN was to cause Neil to play before 800,000 paid attendees, or VN would have to repay the advance. By the time Neil completed his tour, he had only performed before 533,032 paid attendees and GEM demanded a refund. When he refused to pay, GEM sued him.

VN Merchandising conceded that a breach of contract had occurred and the court granted summary judgment for GEM. However, the court refused to grant summary judgment against Vince Neil personally because he did not sign the agreement. Neil proved once again the value of loan-out companies to shield entertainers from personal liability.

Another challenge for musicians, musical groups, and their companies is to stop the flow of the unauthorized use of their names. Elvis Presley Enterprises (EPE) sued Barry Capese for applying the name "The Velvet Elvis" to his Houston, Texas nightclub. In *Elvis Presley Enterprises, Inc. v. Barry Capese*, 141 F.3d 188 (5th Cir. 1998), EPE declared that it was the assignee of all trademarks, copyrights and publicity rights belonging to the Elvis Presley Estate. It asserted that merchandise sales brought in over $20 million in revenue over a five-year period and account for the largest portion of its revenue. *Id.* at 191.

EPE claimed that Capese's nightclub "The Velvet Elvis" infringed its trademarks. While district court held that it was a parody of the mark, the court of appeals disagreed, finding it an infringement and issued an injunction. The court of appeals said that parody was not a defense against trademark infringement, but rather a factor to be considered in determining whether there is a likelihood of infringement. The court of appeals found that "The Velvet Elvis" mark was similar in appearance, sound, and meaning to the Elvis trademarks. *Id.* at 200.

Further, the nightclub had made every effort to link itself to Elvis Presley. Its menu included a frozen drink called "Love Me Blenders" and a hot dog called "Your Football Hound Dog." The nightclub also advertised with slogans such as "The King Lives, " "Viva La Elvis," and "Elvis has not left the building." The court considered these uses as attempts to profit from the good will associated with the Elvis name and trademark. Moreover, these uses were likely to cause consumer confusion and lead consumers to think the Elvis estate officially sponsored them.

Newspapers may sometimes use a trademark name without obtaining permission. The Ninth Circuit permitted News America Publications to use the name of *New Kids on the Block* to conduct a survey asking which one of the New Kids is the most popular. When New Kids sued claiming trademark infringement, the court ruled for the news organization. *See* New Kids on the Block v. News America Publications, Inc. 971 F.2d 302 (9th Cir. 1992). The court noted that the news organization's use did not imply sponsorship or endorsement.

D. PATENT LAW

A patent grants exclusive rights to prohibit others from making, using, and selling the invention to the absolute exclusion of others. It does not give automatically the right to exploit the patent as the patent may be an improvement patent based on another patent.

In which case, the patentee must obtain permission from the other patent holder in order to use his invention based on the other one. The patent term is 17 years from the date of issuance or 20 years from the date of filing.

To patent an invention, the creator must prove that it meets five substantive requirements. First, the invention must be patentable subject matter: under 35 U.S.C. Sec. 501, that is the invention or discovery must be a new and useful process, machine, manufacturer, composition of matter; design, or plant, or it can be a new or useful improvement there of. Second, the invention must be original, which is defined as new. Third, the invention or discovery must fulfill the novelty requirement, which means it is new and was not developed before a certain date. Fourth the invention must be useful, must confer a demonstrated benefit to society and not be illegal, immoral, ineffective, dangerous, merely curious inventions. Finally, the invention or discovery must be non-obvious to those skilled in the arts. There must be synergism so that two plus two equals more than four.

Patented inventions enabled the entertainment industry to grow. One of the most important early patents in the film industry was by Thomas Edison. The famed inventor of the light bulb also created the camera and the movie camera. In *Edison v. American Mutoscope & Biograph Co.*, 151 F. 767 (2d Cir. 1907), Edison sued the Biograph Company for infringing his patent for a kinetographic camera. Although the language of the patent claims was broad enough to cover a camera device, the district court found no infringement because, in considering the practical utility and substantial identity, there were differences in parts, in action, and in result. On appeal, the Second Circuit reversed.

The patent system strikes a bargain similar to the copyright law. It encourages the development of technology, by giving monopoly rights to exploit the invention, while demanding ultimate disclosure of the information to the public. Unlike copyright law where rights accrue once the material is fixed in a tangible means of expression, a patent must be issued from the federal government before the creator obtains these monopoly rights. Patents also differ from trademark law where rights accrue on using the mark in commerce where consumers can purchase the goods.

E. TRADE SECRETS

An old adage proclaims "a secret is only a secret if one of the two parties is dead."[24] Fortunately, death is not a prerequisite to keeping secrets in the entertainment business.

---

[24] Sherri Burr, *Protecting Business Secrets in National and International Commerce,* 17:3 SCIENCE COMMUNICATION 274, 282 (Mar. 1996).

Maintaining undisclosed ideas, information and technology is important to all producers, studios, networks, and recording companies. Towards this end, companies have individuals sign release agreements before sharing ideas. They may also require business partners sign nondisclosure agreements that keep them from revealing business information given to them in confidence. Some high profile celebrities have their pizza delivery boy sign a confidentiality agreement prohibiting him from informing the media about what he learned while briefly in their homes.

Trade secret law protects information that is concealed and gets its value because it is not readily available or known. Initially, courts protected business secrets within their respective jurisdictions on a case-by-case basis using tort theories. This court-made law was eventually expressed in the Restatement of Torts. Forty-five states have adopted Uniform Trade Secrets Act (USTA), sponsored by The National Conference of Commissioners on Uniform Laws, which approved the USTA initially in 1979 and revised it in 1985.

Under the Uniform Trade Secret Act, such information may include "formulas, patterns, compilations, programs, devices, techniques or processes" that

(1) Derives independent economic value (actual or potential) from not being generally known or readily discoverable by proper

means by others who would obtain an economic value from its disclosure or use; and

(2) Is the subject of efforts that are reasonable under the circumstances to maintain its secrecy.

Entertainment companies may consider a variety of information, from plot formulas to special affects, as secrets. The key is to limit disclosures of the information to only those who receive it in confidence. Companies have to keep in mind that there are two types of culprits most likely to steal such secrets: competitors and employees.

The goal of trade secret law is to secure a level playing field among all competitors, who can acquire information through proper means (individual discovery and effort) but not through improper means (theft). With employees, who may someday become competitors, trade secret law seeks to balance the rights of individuals to pursue the knowledge acquired for their careers with the rights of a business to be protected from unfair competition.

The controlling factor is how the person first learned of the information. Even if the information could have been reversed engineered, the fact that it was first learned in confidence will give rise to legal action. By permitting reverse engineering, the law seeks to reward individual efforts, which theft does not.

Once theft has occurred, individuals and companies can seek injunctions, damages and attorneys fees in civil courts. Some states permit criminal sanctions. For federal law, global entertainment companies may rely on The Economic Espionage Act of 1996, which Congress adopted to discourage theft of trade secrets in foreign commerce. This act permits criminal sanctions.

In conclusion, all forms of intellectual property can prove valuable to entertainers, studios and producers. The most recently created form of intellectual property—the right to publicity—will be discussed in Chapter 9, "Celebrity Status."

CHAPTER 6

REPRESENTING ENTERTAINERS

This chapter explores the relationships between entertainers and those who represent them, namely agents, managers, lawyers, and unions. These representatives provide services to entertainers and assist in growing their careers.

The primary job of an agent is to solicit and obtain employment for their clients or material for future exploitation. Entertainers need agents to advance their careers as most studios and production companies will not accept and look at unsolicited manuscripts and projects sent directly from unknown talent. The state of California caps agents' fees at ten percent.

Managers in the film and television industry may assist talent in picking scripts that diversify their abilities. Managers in the music industry may be responsible for everything from running the band to taking care of their tours and personal matters. Managers may receive 5 to 25% of the talent's income. If the manager belongs to a management conglomerate, he may be responsible for several entertainers' careers.

Attorneys draft and review contracts. They may also offer advice on setting up businesses. Some lawyers create pre- and post-nuptial agreements for clients. Others draft their wills and participate in estate planning. Still others may handle criminal matters. When entertainers like Robert Blake and Michael Jackson are charged with crimes, their lawyers must possess special skills in media relations to accompany their understanding of the criminal law.

Unions negotiate agreements with studios and agents that provide minimum fees and working conditions for talent, which are known as minimum basic or collective bargaining agreements. Once they become eligible to join a union such as the Screen Actors Guild, the Directors Guild, the Writers Guild, IATSE, and the American Federation of Musicians, talent must pay membership initiation fees and dues. The challenge for lawyers entering the entertainment law field is to know what the unions have negotiated for their clients so that they do not waste time haggling over rights the talent already possesses.

Entertainers may also have other professionals in their lives, like accountants to manage their finances, and publicists, who assist talent in selling their image. Some publicists specialize in   quieting matters for talent who commit major errors in judgment.

This introduction to the role of representatives sets the stage for the more detailed discussion below. This chapter presents disputes that have arisen about or between talent and their agent, manager, lawyer, and union representatives.

A. AGENTS

William Goldman, the author of *Adventures in the Screen Trade*, writes "[S]tars come and go. Only agents last forever." Goldman, *supra* note 2. Agents endure because the system is set up to guarantee their survival. New film artists may find themselves caught in a paradox—they cannot get work without an agent, and they cannot get an agent to look at them until they demonstrate their talent.

Anyone, including licensed lawyers, seeking to become a talent agent with a conglomerate may have a tough road ahead. Typically, the big agencies like Creative Artist Agency, International Creative Management, United Talent Agency, and William Morris, hire and place recruits in the mailroom sorting the incoming correspondence and making deliveries. After succeeding in the mailroom job, they may move on to become desk and personal assistants to other agents. This apprentice rotation can take two years before the recruit becomes an assistant agent or full agent.

Wally Amos,[25] who would later become renowned for launching "Famous Amos Cookies," began his agent career earning $50 a week as a trainee in the mailroom of the William Morris Agency in 1961. WALLY AMOS AND EDEN-LEE MURRAY, THE COOKIE NEVER CRUMBLES 37 (2001). In his book, *Man With No Name*, Amos describes his initial duties as "sorting mail and running errands." WALLY AMOS, MAN WITH NO NAME 43 (1994).

Amos immersed himself in learning about the business and within two months was promoted to substitute secretary. By the end of his first year, he was elevated to talent agent and became the founding member of a new rock and roll division. He brought in Simon and Garfunkel when they were unknown and playing in small clubs. In his five and a half years as an agent, he also booked and promoted The Supremes, The Temptations, Dionne Warwick, Helen Reddy, and Marvin Gaye. *Id.* at 44-45. For Amos, a perk to becoming an agent, i.e., the opportunity to fraternize with available women, turned into a pitfall. He divorced twice during these years.

---

[25] The author initially met Mr. Amos when he spoke to her Intellectual Property Class at the University of Hawaii in November 1998. She then interviewed him for the premier of the television show *Arts Talk* in January 1999 on Olelo Channel 52 in Honolulu, Hawaii.

The current economic rewards associated with succeeding as an agent are potentially huge with income exceeding $1 million a year, as one Los Angeles agent privately said. The downsides are equally enormous. This agent said that he fields over 100 calls and 125 e-mails daily. A desk assistant sits in his office to make and receive phone calls, and to do instant fact checking. Sometimes while he is on the phone with one person, he will have his desk assistant call another agent to verify the truth of what the person on the phone is telling him. He said it is harder for others to lie to him because he has access to a wealth of knowledge.

He confessed that other downsides are the long hours and his inability to take more than two or three days off from work at a time. When he travels to nice places like the Cannes Film Festival, he works. This agent was also aware that no matter how much effort he contributes to building an artist's career, the artist might leave him at any moment for another agent. When asked whether a gentlemen's agreement keeps agents from poaching each other's clients, he barked, "You steal from us; we steal from you."

For many individuals, the rewards of becoming an agent are worth the risks. Over the years, California and New York have passed legislation regulating agents. California talent agents are regulated by the California Labor Law code, a few provisions of which are reprinted below, and by the Screen Actors Guild to the extent that they represent film artists.

Section 1700.4 of the California Labor Code defines talent agents and artists as follows:

> (a) "Talent agency" means a person or corporation who engages in the occupation of procuring, offering, promising, or attempting to procure employment or engagements for an artist or artists, except that the activities of procuring, offering, or promising to procure recording contracts for an artist or artists shall not of itself subject a person or corporation to regulation and licensing under this chapter. Talent agencies may, in addition, counsel or direct artists in the development of their professional careers.

> (b) "Artists" means actors and actresses rendering services on the legitimate stage and in the production of motion pictures, radio artists, musical artists, musical organizations, directors of legitimate stage, motion picture and radio productions, musical directors, writers, cinematographers, composers, lyricists, arrangers, models, and other artists and persons rendering professional services in motion picture, theatrical, radio, television and other entertainment enterprises.

Cal. Lab. Code § 1700.4 (2003), "Talent agency"; "Artists." One of the goals of the Talent Agencies Act is to prevent improper persons from becoming talent agents and to regulate such activity for the protection of the public.

The entire Talent Agencies Act, Lab. Code, §§ 1700-1700.47, is considered a remedial statute designed to protect artists and correct abuses, which have been the subject of both legislative action and judicial decision. The act voids contracts between an unlicensed agent and an artist. *See* Waisbren v. Peppercorn Productions, Inc., 48 Cal. Rptr. 2d 437 (Cal. App. 2 Dist. 1995).

In *Waisbren v. Peppercorn Productions*, Inc., a personal manager sued his former client, a company specialized in the design and creation of puppets for use in the entertainment industry, for breach of contract and for failure to pay him a percentage of its profits. In return for managing certain business affairs and occasionally procuring employment for Peppercorn, Waisbren was to receive 15 percent of its profits. After Peppercorn terminated its relationship with him, Waisbren filed suit to recover unpaid amounts.

The California Court of Appeals distinguished an agent's duties to procure employment from a manager's responsibilities to advise and direct artists in the development of their careers. *Id.* at 438. The court concluded that because Waisbren had functioned as a talent agent, by procuring employment for Peppercorn, he was required to be licensed under the Talent Agencies Act. The court affirmed the trial court's voiding of the parties' oral agreement because Waisbren had not obtained the necessary license under the Talent Agencies Act.

New York rules regulating agents also apply to booking agents who secure lectures and engagements for film and theater clients. In *Friedkin v. Walker*, 90 Misc.2d 680, 395 N.Y.S.2d 611 (N.Y. City Civ. Ct. 1977), director William Friedkin (*The French Connection, The Exorcist*) sued Harry Walker, seeking the return of $4,743.32 in commissions. As an unlicensed agent, Walker managed, directed and promoted lectures, talks and addresses by well-known personalities. He charged Friedkin a 30% commission to secure lecture engagements. Although he booked 23, Friedkin only performed three and paid commissions on those. The court ruled in Friedkin's favor because Walker was an unlicensed agent.

A properly licensed agent must be careful how she engages employment for talent. Director Stephen Frears (*The Grifters, Dirty Pretty Things*) had an agent accept money and commit him to a picture before he had reviewed the script. *See* Burr and Henslee, *supra* note 1, at 109. After he read the script, he realized the film wasn't for him and decided to back out of his oral agreement. His attorney advised him that he might have a claim against his agent for taking the money. He learned from that experience that "[t]aking money creates a contract and expectations that you are really going to do the picture." *Id.*

Actor Kelsey Grammer experienced the opposite problem with his agent. He became dissatisfied with his representatives at The Artist Agency because they failed to secure film work for him. His two television shows, *Cheers* and *Frasier*, were obtained before he joined the Artist Agency. He sought freedom from his agreement with Artist Agency by negotiating an interim deal whereby Artist Agency would continue to represent him on his television projects and he could seek other representation on film deals. After a year, Grammer terminated his relationship with the Artist Agency. The Agency then sued him for $2 million in back commissions. A three-member arbitration panel decided in favor of the Agency.

When Grammer appealed, the federal district court and court of appeals affirmed. In *Grammer v. Artists Agency*, 287 F.3d 886 (9th Cir. 2002), the actor argued that his interim contracts violated SAG Rule 16(g) § IV(C)(1), which provides that all "contracts ... not complying with these Regulations ... shall be void except as hereafter provided." SAG initially rejected the interim contract but eventually accepted it after the Artist Agency faxed a copy of the settlement agreement to prove the interim contract was in the best interest of Grammer. The arbitration panel found that Grammer had waived the Rule 16(g) violations and the courts agreed.

Grammer turned his problems with agents into humor. From *Frasier's* earliest beginnings in 1993 until its conclusion in 2004, actress Harriet Sansom Harris hammed up the recurring character Bebe Glazer as an unscrupulous agent who would do anything for money and to advance her own interests. Bebe's shenanigans were often to the detriment of her client's welfare.

B. MANAGERS

What exactly are the responsibilities of an artist manager? According to the court in *Raden v. Lauri*, one is not an artist's manager unless he advises, counsels and directs artists in the development of their professional careers...." 20 Cal. App.2d 778, 262 P.2d 61, 64 (Cal. Ct. App. 1953).

The jobs of the agents and managers may overlap when managers begin securing employment for their clients. As indicated in the *Waisbren* and *Friedkin* cases, managers risk not being paid when they act as an agent without procuring the appropriate license.

In *Wachs v. Curry*, 13 Cal.App.4th 616, 16 Cal.Rptr.2d 496 (Cal. Ct. App. 1993), Wachs and X Management Inc. lost its suit against actor and television host Arsenio Hall. The parties' personal management contract required

Hall to pay 15% of his earnings from all of his activities in the entertainment industry. Despite the contract's statement that Wachs had not promised to obtain employment or engagements for him, the company did so. Hall successfully sought the return of all moneys collected from him and his employers in connection with his activities in the entertainment industry.

The court in *Wachs v. Curry* discussed the California Talent Act's exemption of recording contracts. The California Entertainment Commission recommended the exemption permitting managers to secure a recording contract for a musician because "[i]n the recording industry, many successful artists retain personal managers to act as their intermediaries, and negotiations for a recording contract are commonly conducted by a personal manager, not a talent agent." *Id.* at 625. The Commission also observed that the "managers frequently contribute financial support for the living and business expenses of entertainers. They may act as a conduit between the artist and the recording company." *Id.*

In *Buchwald v. Superior Court*, 254 Cal.App.2d 347, 62 Cal.Rptr. 364 (Cal. Ct. App. 1967), the musical group Jefferson Airplane sued their personal manager Matthew Katz. Their written agreement stated that Katz had not agreed to obtain employment for the group and that he was not authorized to do so. *Id.* at 351. Jefferson Airplane claimed that, despite the contractual language, Katz did indeed procure bookings for them. Katz argued that the written agreement established that he was not subject to statutory regulation.

The court rejected Katz's contention. It looked to the illegality lying behind the contract to determine whether the contract was prohibited. *Id.* at 355. *Buchwald* held generally that procurement efforts require a license and that the substance of the parties' relationship, not its form, is controlling. *See* Waisbren v. Peppercorn Productions, Inc., 48 Cal.Rptr.2d 437 (Cal. Ct. App. 1995).

The *Waisbren* court noted that when *Buchwald* was decided, Labor Code section 1700.4 used the term "artists' manager" instead of "talent agency" and was part of the Artists' Managers Act, *see* Stats.1959, ch. 888, § 1, pp. 2921, 2922. Waisbren, 48 Cal. Rptr. 2d at 442, n.7. The 1959 Statute defined an "artists' manager" as "a person who engages in the occupation of advising, counseling, or directing artists in the development or advancement of their professional careers and who procures, offers, promises or attempts to procure employment or engagements for an artist...." (Stats.1959, ch. 888, § 1, p. 2921.) In 1978, the Legislature changed the name of the statutory scheme and amended section 1700.4 to use the term "talent agency." (Stats.1978, ch. 1382, §§ 3, 6, pp. 4575, 4576.) These changes did not alter the statute's remedial. Waisbren, 48 Cal. Rptr. 2d at 442, n.7.

While managers lost the regulatory battle that would have permitted them to procure employment for artists, the Los Angeles Times reported in 1998 that agents were becoming obsolete. *See* Amy Wallace, *Hollywood Agents Lose the Throne*, L.A. TIMES, Dec. 11, 1998. Wallace's article noted that many agents were turning themselves into personal managers whereby they could charge a higher fee, 15% instead of 10% of the client's earnings. She also observed that some of the biggest stars don't have agents. She said that Leonardo DiCaprio and Jackie Chan were represented solely by managers, and that "Kevin Costner and Sharon Stone use lawyers to close deals." *Id.*

C. LAWYERS

In an interview, Academy Award-winning actress Shirley MacLaine stressed the importance of lawyers to the success of actors. She said, "Actresses and actors don't worry too much about the law. Their lawyers and agents do that. When actresses hire lawyers, they expect the lawyers to do everything. We usually just follow their recommendations." Burr & Henslee, *supra* note 1, at 258.

To work in the entertainment industry, it is helpful if the lawyer acquires knowledge about corporate and business law, tax law, labor law, intellectual property, criminal law, family law, contracts, and immigration. While lawyers typically begin their career at a studio on the legal side, some may move to the business side if they demonstrate sufficient skill. Studio lawyers are paid a salary, while law firms may charge hourly fees or by the job. In some instances, lawyers enter into contracts to do all the talent's legal work (including contracts, divorces, adoptions, wills, and criminal defense) in return for 5% of the talent's gross dollar revenue.

In his law review article, Gary E. Devlin notes that contemporary lawyers in the entertainment industry have been known to package deals, shop talent and creative material, and advise on financial matters, thereby crossing over into the definitional realms of agent and manager. At the same time, the personal manager has evolved into a powerful force, commanding up to twenty percent of an artist's gross income and obtaining production credit that result in fees from studios. Agents are thereby left to attend to the one glaring need that managers cannot fulfill due to the provisions of the Act--procuring employment for artists. Gary E. Devlin, *The Talent Agencies Act: Reconciling the Controversies Surrounding Lawyers, Managers, and Agents Participating in California's Entertainment*, 28 PEPPER. L. REV. 381 (2001).

Among the challenges that lawyers face in representing clients in the entertainment industry is dealing with strong egos. When asked on the cable television show *Arts Talk* what was the most difficult aspect of being an entertainment lawyer, Johnnie Cochran replied,

"Having to say no to people who are not used to having people say no to them."[26]

From the client viewpoint, screenwriter Duncan North says, "Lawyers and agents are not [our] spiritual mentors. But if they are really, really good, then they make it easier for [us] to be that way." *Id.* at 144. He defines good attorneys as those who "most assiduously fight" for their clients' rights. *Id.*

Author and screenwriter Max Evans says his long-term lawyer Norma Fink has "never had a client that doesn't honor her as if she's a bishop. "She's mean to me," he says. "She's mean to everybody. She's just mean. But the point of it is she's going to be mean for you. There's no way a studio can buy her out or intimidate her. She has a very powerful clientele." *Id.* at 143.

D. UNIONS

In the film and television industries, the Screen Actors Guild (SAG), The Directors Guild of America (DGA), The Writers Guild of America (WGA), and the International Alliance of Theatrical Stage Employees (IATSE) are the major unions that represent actors, directors, screenwriters, and crew respectively. They negotiate minimum basic agreements with

---

[26] *ARTS TALK* (Comcast Channel 27 television broadcast, January 31, 2000).

studios and producers to obtain minimum scale wages, acceptable working conditions, creative rights, and credits for their members. The American Federation of Musicians negotiates master agreements with symphony orchestras and Actors Equity negotiates with Broadway producers on behalf of talent.

Who is bound by guild agreements? In *Hollywood Online* (1996), Allen R. Grogan and Sam C. Mandel wrote the following:

> Guild agreements are contracts. Typically, they bind guild members and producer signatories to the agreement.... Once the producer is a signatory to a guild agreement, he or she may hire members of that guild to provide services.... Furthermore, although the exact rules will differ with each guild agreement, most guild agreements contain cross-affiliation provisions which, in the case of an individual producer signatory, bind not only the individual but also all companies controlled by such individual and in the case of a corporate signatory, bind all subsidiaries of such entity....

Unions are now trying to organize reality TV shows. Because television series like *The Bachelor* and *Survivor* are not unionized, they do not pay scale wages, do not provide insurance, and do not entitle participants, writers, and directors to residuals, unless specifically negotiated. *See* Jim Rendon, *Unions*

Aim to Share in the Success of Reality TV, N.Y. TIMES, Jan. 25, 2004, at Business, P.4.   The following subsections discuss issues that have arisen with each of the guilds.

1. SCREEN ACTORS GUILD

SAG's Global Rule One requires, "No member shall work as a performer or make an agreement to work as a performer for any producer who has not executed a basic minimum agreement with the Guild which is in full force and effect." SAG warns members that they "lose Pension & Health benefits, residuals payments, work safety, and other protections from SAG when they work without a SAG contract." *See* http://www.sag.org/sag-WebApp/index.jsp.

SAG also negotiates limited exhibition agreements, which, depending on the size of the production budget, permit producers flexibility. At a production budget of less than $75,000, producers may defer salaries. With a $200,000 production budget, they pay significantly lower rates. For a $500,000 production budget, producers may cover a fewer number of background actors. SCREEN ACTORS GUILD, FILM CONTRACTS DIGEST 2-6 (2003).   In other words, the size of the production budget determines the minimum fees that the actors get paid. For a production budget of less than $2,000,000 effective July 1, 2003, a general background actor must receive a minimum of $115, a day performer must receive $466, and a weekly performer $1,620. *Id.* at 9-10.

Conflict can arise if an actor or actress accepts a part before joining SAG or paying her SAG dues. Part-time actress Naomi Marquez accepted a one-line role in an episode of the television series *Medicine Ball.* Lakeside Productions, a signatory to SAG collective bargaining agreement, produced the show. Lakeside called SAG to confirm Marquez's eligibility and was advised that she needed to pay her union dues. After Marquez learned that her dues would be $500, she tried to negotiate with SAG to permit payment of her dues after she received compensation for her film work. Because she had not resolved her conflict with SAG the day before her appearance, Lakeside recast the role. SAG later faxed a letter saying it did not object to Marquez playing the part, but it arrived too late. Marquez then sued SAG and Lakeside.

In *Marquez v. Screen Actors Guild*, 525 U.S. 33 (1998), Marquez alleged that SAG breached its duty of fair representation under National Labor Relations Act (NLRA) by negotiating and enforcing flawed union security clause and by failing to notify her truthfully about her NLRA rights. Marquez argued that SAG should have provided and notified her of a 30-day grace period following her new employment before she was required to pay her dues. The Supreme Court disagreed, holding that SAG had not breached its duty of fair representation. Its union security clause appropriately tracked the language of §8(a)(3) of the NLRA.

2. DIRECTOR'S GUILD

The DGA negotiates working conditions and minimum salaries for directors depending on the size of the budget. From July 1, 2003 to June 30, 2004, employers were required to pay a minimum weekly salary of $8,150 for low budget films (up to $500,000), $9,263 for medium budget films ($500,000 to $1.5 million) and $12,969 for high budget films (that exceed $1.5 million).

The size of the budget also determines minimum salary scale for preparation and post-production editing time. Like SAG, the DGA announces annual awards recognizing the talent of its members. According to the DGA website, http://www.dga.org/index2.php3, only six times between 1949 and 2003 has the winner of the DGA Award not gone on to win the Best Director Oscar®.

Labor unions frequently bring legal actions to enforce their members' contracts. The Directors Guild of America sued Millennium Television Network when it failed to pay several directors for their work in a 1999 New Year's Eve telecast called "Millennium World Broadcast." Directors Guild of America v. Millennium Television Network, 2001 WL 1744609 (C.D. Cal. 2001). The district court found that because the directors did perform the work and labored on the telecast, they were owed payment for their services, despite the fact that Millennium cancelled the show on December 23, 1999. An arbitrator awarded the directors $64,846.13 in compensation and $14,864.65 in pension/health contributions, plus late charges.

In this action, DGA also sued Frontier Insurance Company (Frontier) NAC Reinsurance Corporation (NAC). DGA argued that these two companies were liable for the arbitration award obtained against Millennium, which went out of business. Frontier and NAC had executed a payment bond with Millennium making them liable as co-sureties to "any and all persons, corporations who perform work or labor on" the "Millennium World Broadcast" scheduled for December 31, 1999." *Id.*

In its defense, NAC argued the express terms of the bond do not encompass the plaintiffs' arbitration award against Millenium because they did not actually "perform work or labor on" the cancelled telecast. NAC also argued that plaintiffs failed to mitigate their damages following the cancellation of the telecast. The district court, however, disagreed with this argument. It found that the plaintiffs had "performed work" or "labored on" the telecast and were therefore owed the amounts set forth in the arbitration award. It granted DGA's motion for summary judgment. *Id.* at *6.

3. WRITERS GUILD OF AMERICA

The Writers Guild has two divisions, the Writers Guild East and the Writers Guild West, who divide the country along the Mississippi River. The WGA West represents screenwriters who live west of river. Under the contract that both Guilds negotiated in 2001, screenwriters receive a minimum of $50,100 for an original screenplay, including treatment. WRITERS GUILD, SCHEDULE OF MINIMUMS (May 2, 2003).

Since the WGA represents employees, you have to be employed before you can join and yet the signatories are limited to hiring only WGA members. To evade this catch-22, new screenwriters must find someone who wants to buy their script and is willing to sign the minimum basic agreement. In the event of a dispute over which screenwriters are entitled to credit on a film, the WGA will arbitrate the dispute and award credit. An ampersand (&) indicates two writers wrote the script as a joint work; a written "and" indicates writers who worked independently of each other.

The WGA sometimes allocates screen credits after 17 writers contributed to a screenplay. Greg Brooker, who became one of two credited writers on *Stuart Little*, said, "A lot of [the 17 writers] were brought in to write a line or two for the animals.... You could say that *Stuart Little* was written by committee.   After we went through the Writers Guild credit arbitration, only two writers received credit: me and M.

Night Shyamalan. I was the first writer, and he was the third. I spent a lot of time writing my letter to the WGA explaining how I created my screenplay and what was mine. I didn't claim the whole picture because the concept changed." Burr and Henslee, *supra* note 1, at 165.

According to screenwriter Walon Green (*The Wild Bunch, Eraser*),

> "The Writers Guild is a mixed blessing for writers. The WGA performs legal services that writers cannot afford to do on their own. The contract that the WGA has with the studios allows them to decide things like credit arbitration. I've arbitrated four times and lost once. Only three of my 13 credited films went through arbitration. Arbitration can occur in strange ways. I'm adapting a book now that has been through three prior screenplay adaptations. While I haven't seen the prior adaptations, it's possible that we will all have similar scenes since we are working from the book. This is the kind of situation that could easily end in arbitration to determine who is entitled to the credit for writing the film."

Burr and Henslee, *supra* note 1, at 19-20.

When writers are unhappy with the results of the arbitration process, they can bring legal action. Nick Marino sued the WGA, Francis Coppola, and Mario Puzo, charging that the arbitration procedures used to determine the screenwriting credit to *Godfather III* were fundamentally unfair. Marino v. WGA, 992 F.2d 1480 (9th Cir. 1993). Marino objected to the WGA practice of keeping the arbitrators' identities confidential and he claimed that WGA breached its duties of fair representation.

In 1985, Marino co-wrote with Thomas Wright a treatment for *Godfather III*, which Paramount Pictures Corporation purchased and then hired Marino to write a screenplay based on his treatment. Marino completed the screenplay in 1985, but Paramount chose not to produce it at that time. In 1987, Marino wrote a second treatment and sent it unsolicited to executives at a production studio owned by Coppola. They did not purchase Marino's 1987 treatment. In 1989 and 1990, Coppola and Puzo co-wrote a screenplay for *Godfather III*, which was produced and completed in 1990. Prior to the film's release, Marino was notified that WGA would be conducting an arbitration to determine the writing credits for *Godfather III*. Accordingly, Marino, Coppola and Puzo submitted written materials and statements for review.

The court of appeals outlined the three stages of the WGA arbitration process. In the first phase, a committee conducts a hearing to decide disputes as to "authenticity, identification, sequence, authorship or completeness of any literary material to be considered." *Id.* at 1482. These arbiters, whose names are kept confidential from the writers, the public, and each other, conduct the second phase. The three arbiters individually read material submitted by the film company and the writers to decide who is entitled to screen credit. A majority vote decides the issue. The third phase is conducted by a Policy Review Board (PRB) who hear requests from writers concerned that there has been a dereliction in duty by the arbiters or that they have misinterpreted, misapplied or violated WGA policies. The court notes that the entire process must occur with 21 business days or the producer's own selection may become final. *Id.*

On November 5, 1990, the WGA informed Marino that Coppola and Puzo would receive sole writing credit. Marino requested a hearing before the PRB where he objected to the arbitration procedure. *Id.* at 1482. The PRB telephoned the three arbiters and presented Marino's allegations to them. The PRB discovered that one arbiter had not read Marino's 1985 treatment. That arbiter was sent the 1985 treatment for review, and the arbiter then reaffirmed the prior conclusion. The PRB subsequently informed Marino that a new arbitration was unnecessary and that the arbitration decision was final.

The court of appeals found that Marino had waived his right to object to the arbitration proceedings by his failure to protest the procedure before arbiters were selected and performed their task. The court of appeals also concluded that Marino had failed to establish that the union breached its duty of fair representation in its conduct of arbitration proceedings.

4. IATSE

IATSE's full name is the International Alliance of Theatrical Stage Employees, Moving Picture Technicians, Artists and Allied Crafts of the United States, Its Territories and Canada. IATSE was formed more than a century ago to represent film technicians. With a membership of over 104,000 members, IATSE boasts that it is the largest labor union in the entertainment and related industries. *See* http://www.iatse-intl.org/about/welcome.html.

On January 1, 2004, IATSE completed negotiations with companies such as Intermedia Films, Miramax Pictures, and New Line Pictures, to increase the low budget cap from $7 million to $8.5 million to give producers more operating flexibility and in return the producers would improve rest periods and meal provisions. *See* http://www.iatse-intl.org/index_html.html.

IATSE has also been sued for failure to provide fair representation. Michael Wills and Robert Thurlwell charged in *Wills v. Walt Disney Pictures and Television*, 173 F.3d 862 (9th Cir. 1998), that IATSE unfairly represented them in their dispute with Disney. Wills and Thurlwell claimed that Disney employed fewer senior craft services workers in violation of the collective bargaining agreement and that Thurlwell had been unfairly terminated after the dispute arose.

The court of appeals said that to establish a union breached its duty of fair representation, the employee "must show that the union's conduct toward him was 'arbitrary, discriminatory, or in bad faith'." To be arbitrary, the union's conduct must lack a rational basis, and show "egregious disregard" for the rights of its members. *Id.*

The court of appeals split its decision. It first held that IATSE did not breach its duty in failing to follow-up on Wills and Thurlwell's claim that they were discriminated against because of age. After investigating, the union determined that the two men were unavailable when the initial craft positions were filled on *In the Army Now.* When a junior worker filled a later available position that the two men could have taken, the union negotiated a $400 settlement on their behalf.

Second, the court of appeals decided that IATSE did breach its duty by not pursuing the issue of whether Thurlwell resigned, as Disney contended, or was fired, as he maintained. The court decided that the IATSE representative should have followed up to determine how Thurlwell had left after working 30 years for Disney. The court affirmed the summary judgment on the age discrimination issue and reversed on the resignation claim.

5. AMERICAN FEDERATION OF MUSICIANS

The American Federation of Musicians (AFM) was founded in 1896 to improve the professional lives of musicians. The union considers any individual who receives pay for his musical services as a professional musician. Within its first ten years, the AFM represented 45,000 musicians throughout North America. It currently has approximately 251 local chapters, representing over 100,000 members. The local chapters negotiate with management on behalf of the musicians.

"Our basic reason for existing is to protect the interest of musicians in the working field," says Larry Wheeler, president of the New Mexico branch of the AFM, Local #618. The cost to join AFM depends on where the musician is located. The New Mexico local charges musicians $60 to join the federal union, $20 to join the local union and $95 for yearly dues. Wheeler says, "The main benefit is that musicians have local representation if they believe they are unduly let go." He also says that the union makes available individual contracts and represents union members to produce collective bargaining agreements with management. Among other activities, the AFM and its locals file grievances and/or lawsuits against symphonies on behalf of their members.

In *American Federation of Musicians v. St. Louis Symphony*, 203 F.3d 1079 (8th Cir. 2000), the union brought an action in the district court to compel the symphony to arbitrate a grievance pursuant to the parties' collective bargaining agreement. The union was granted its motion for summary judgment but was denied its motion for attorneys' fees. The Eight Circuit affirmed.

The dispute arose after violist Louis Kampouis, who had initially been hired to perform in 1949, was informed on September 2, 1997, when he reported to work that he could no longer rehearse or perform with the orchestra. Kampouris, who was 68 at the time, sued the symphony for age discrimination and intentional infliction of emotional distress after it discontinued his salary and benefits. *Id.* at 1080.

The Eight Circuit affirmed the denial of attorneys' fees because the union's proposed arbitration panel included arbitrators from outside the St. Louis metropolitan area. In a different arbitration, the union and symphony had agreed to limit themselves to local arbiters. The court found that the symphony's reliance on the previous agreement was not unreasonable.

Allen Chase claimed that the Detroit Symphony Orchestra fired him from his position as a trombonist because of his participation in union activities. Chase rejected an offer of a $10 a week raise by telling the orchestra's general manager, "Get yourself another boy. I do not accept." Michigan Employment Relations

Commission v. Detroit Symphony Orchestra, 393 Mich. 116, 119, 223 N.W.2d 283 (Mich. Sup. Ct. 1974). Contacted a week later, he indicated he had not changed his mind. The orchestra declared the position vacant and began auditioning for a new trombonist. When Chase eventually tried to accept the offer, he was told it was withdrawn. He auditioned for the vacancy but was not rehired.

Chase charged that the orchestra had discharged him because of his union animus. The trial examiner disagreed. After conducting an evidentiary hearing and listening to testimony from the parties, he concluded that Chase quit the orchestra when he rejected the contract and the raise with the abrupt, "Get yourself another boy." *Id.* The Michigan Employment Relations Commission (MERC) Board reversed the trial examiner's ruling, finding there was union animus. The Michigan Court of Appeals reversed the MERC board and the Michigan Supreme Court affirmed, concluding that the MERC Board's finding was not supported by "substantial evidence." *Id.* at 121.

In summary, agents, managers, lawyers, and unions play a vital role in the entertainment industry. They assist entertainers in achieving their goal, and sometimes are sued by entertainers for failure to represent them in a fair manner. Chapter 7 will address in more detail the issues of credits and compensation, which representatives negotiate for and on behalf of talent.

CHAPTER 7

CREDIT & COMPENSATION

Credit and compensation issues intertwine in the entertainment industry. Credit accords recognition to the talent who contributes to the final product. Talent is then compensated according to the value of his or her work. This chapter will discuss the importance of credit and the intricacies of the compensation system in the film, television, and music industries.

A. CREDIT

In the publishing industry, the placing of the author's name on the book is supposed to indicate who penned the manuscript. However, for the book *It Takes a Village*, former First Lady Hilary Clinton received sole author credit, although Barbara Feinman Todd ghostwrote it. While Feinman Todd was compensated for her services, there was no indication anywhere within the manuscript of her contributions to the book, which became a bestseller. Had Feinman Todd received direct credit, those who liked the book might have looked up other works that she wrote and increased her sales.

Credit is important because the person receives acknowledgement for his or her contributions, and it can lead to increased compensation. Dan Brown wrote *Angels & Demons* before *The Da Vinci Code*, but it was only after the latter became a runaway bestseller that the former climbed to the top of bestseller lists.

The same phenomenon happens throughout the entertainment industry. A film artist who hits it big in one film will create demand for her former and future movies. Television actor Kelsey Grammar began performing the Frasier character on *Cheers* in 1984. After the demise of that sitcom in 1993, he starred in the show *Frasier* from 1993 to 2004. By sticking with the same character for 20 years, he tied James Arness, who starred as Matt Dillon on *Gunsmoke*, for playing the longest ongoing TV character. Similarly, in the music industry, musicians want to receive credit for the notes they write and sing.

1. FILM CREDITS

Crediting talent for their contributions was a slow developing concept in the film industry. During the era of silent films, studios did not indicate which actors starred in their films. According to William Goldman, if fans wanted to write actors, they sent letters to "The Butler with the Mustache" or "The Girl with the Curly Blonde Hair." Goldman, *supra* note 2, at 5. Viewers saw only the name of the film and the production companies until the companies recognized that giving credit improved the selling of films, as audience members were likely to return to see a particular actor in his next picture. Similarly, if viewers liked the writing in *Casablanca* they might rush out to see *Arsenic & Old Lace* once they realized that Julius J. Epstein penned both pictures.

Currently, at the beginning and end of films, the credits roll or blink in and out on screen. Credit refers to the listing of a person's name next to the function he or she performed in the entertainment project. The "story by" credit indicates the person who developed the story but did not write the screenplay. That credit is denoted as "written by" and may go to one or more people. An ampersand (&) indicates two or more writers who worked together to create a joint work. The word "and" designates two or more authors who contributed to the script after the first author had finished the original script. The "script supervisor" took detailed notes (scene number, take number, camera position, & dialogue running time) during the filming, which aids the director and editor in deciding which cuts to add to the final product.

Depending on the size of the project and the amount of special effects, several hundred credits may scroll across the screen at the end. The last three credits at the beginning of the film are usually the producer, the writer, and the director. The director credit may also be the first credit listed on screen at the beginning of the movie, such as "A film by Alfred Hitchcock" or "A Spike Lee Joint." While national audiences tend to depart when the credits commence, L.A. audiences often stay to the last frame, usually as the copyright indicator is shown. This occurs out of deference to those who participated in the venture.

Credits have both financial and psychological consequences. Talent and crew find that their pay rises as their credit increases from "Best Boy or Girl" (first assistant electrician who adjust lighting) to "Gaffer" (chief electrician) or from "Grip" (a laborer who creates and breaks down stage sets) to "Key Grip" (the head of the crew). Further, pay increases as the talent's reputation for producing excellent work in the industry grows. Likewise, the psychological reward comes from the acknowledgement of the person's role in the project, that no matter how small the task may have been, it added value to the film.

Billing, which relates to order of credit placement, is particularly important to actors as their stature may be based on whether their name is placed before or after the title of the film. In *Smithers v. MGM Studios*, the court said that billing "reflects the actor's stature in the industry, and affects his negotiations for roles, since it reflects what his status and compensation has been in the past. Billing reflects recognition by the producer and the public of the actor's importance or 'star quality,' and in turn affects the author's compensation in present an future roles." 139 Cal. App. 3d 643, 189 Cal. Rptr. 20, 23 (Cal. App. Ct. 1983). If the actress is not the star, the sooner her name appears after the star the better, unless the actor receives the final listing, such as "and starring Catherine Zeta-Jones."

For some actors, billing issues can generate lawsuits. Sophia Loren sued Samuel Bronston Productions for breaching an agreement that required "in all paid advertising of 'El Cid' Miss. Loren is to be accorded 'second (2nd) star billing above the title, 100% the same size and type of the title on the same line, same size, same prominence as that used for Charlton Heston, who received first (1st) star billing'." Sophia Loren v. Samuel Bronston Productions, 32 Misc. 2d 602, 224 N.Y.S. 2d 959 (N.Y. Supreme Ct. 1962). Ms. Loren claimed the production company violated the agreement by placing her name below that of Charlton Heston on electrically illuminated upright signs. The defendants claimed that this was in keeping with the billing clause.

The court agreed, questioning whether Loren was "really in danger of suffering the loss of prestige and other damage attributed to [the] non-observance" of the agreement. *Id.* at 604. While the judge scheduled the dispute for trial, he made clear how he was leaning in the opening paragraph of his opinion when he used words such as "egocentricity" and "vanity" to refer to Miss. Loren. He indicated that such vanity was

> "due in measurable part to the adulation
> which the public showers on the denizens of
> the entertainment world in a profusion
> wholly disproportionate to the intrinsic
> contribution which they make to the scheme
> of things when seen in correct perspective.
> For that matter often in disproportionate to
> any true talent, latent or apparent."

Id. at 602. Since there are no further references
to this case, it likely settled before trial.

The unions have a say in credit issues. SAG
negotiates minimum credit requirements for
actors, who can by contract negotiate for size
and placement of the credit. The Writers Guild
also establishes minimum requirements to
receive a screenwriter's credit. When several
screenwriters contribute to the final movie, the
WGA arbitrates to determine who is entitled to
receive the writing credit. Screenwriter Walon
Green (*Eraser, Dinosaur, The Hi-Lo Country*)
says,

> "I've arbitrated four times and lost once.
> Only three of my 13 credited films went
> through arbitration. Arbitration can occur in
> strange ways. I'm adapting a book now that
> has been through three prior screenplay
> adaptations. While I haven't seen the prior
> adaptations, it's possible that we will all
> have similar scenes since we are working
> from the book. This is the kind of situation
> that could easily end in arbitration to

> determine who is entitled to the credit for
> writing the film."

Burr and Henslee, *supra* note 1, at 20. The
arbitration to determine who is entitled to credit
is done before the release of the film, although a
lawsuit may occur after the release, particularly
if the film is a hit.

Sometimes directors and writers seek to
limit their credit on films they deem unworthy.
The Wall Street Journal reported in 1996 that
directors hide behind the pseudonym Alan
Smithee to disassociate themselves from a dud.
Director David Lynch substituted the name
"Alan Smithee" for his own when his *Dune* was
re-cut to appear on television. *See* Eben
Shapiro, *Movies: Despite Disdain, a Legendary
Director Endures*, WALL ST. J., Apr. 19, 1996, at
B1.

When Tristar Pictures cut 22 minutes from
the film *Thunderheart* starring Val Kilmer to
show it on commercial television, the director
Michael Apted objected and requested his name
be removed. *See* Tristar v. Director's Guild of
America, 160 F.3d 537 (9th Cir. 1997). Section
8-211 of the DGA's collective bargaining
agreement with Tristar entitled the director to a
pseudonym if he persuaded the DGA's
Director's Council. The Council, an arbitrator,
and the courts ruled in Apted's favor. When
Tristar aired *Thunderheart* on Fox, it carried the
label "An Adam Smithy Film." *Id.* at 539

In 1992, Stephen King sought an injunction to prohibit the use of his name in connection with the film adaptation of *The Lawnmower Man*. King wrote a short story by the same title in 1970 and assigned the motion picture and television rights to Great Fantastic Picture Corporation in 1978. In 1990, Great Fantastic transferred its rights to Allied, a London production company, which set about making a picture it described as "Stephen King's The Lawnmower Man," thus according King possessory credit. King v. Innovation Books, 976 F.2d 824 (2nd Cir. 1992).

King learned of the picture in early October 1991 from a film magazine article and protested the possessory credit given him in a letter dated October 9, 1991, and stated that he did not want this credit. He objected to the possessory credit as a misrepresentation since the film was very different from his short story. On May 20, 1992, King expressed concern that the "based upon credit," which usually indicates the original source of the film material, was misleading. In his lawsuit, King claimed that both credits violated Sec. 43(a) of the Lanham Act, which prohibits false designation of origin.

The district court agreed and granted an initial injunction prohibiting both credits. It concluded that "the possessory credit was false on its face [and] that the "based upon" credit was misleading." *Id.* at 828. The court of appeals let stand the possessor credit injunction, but overturned the injunction as to the "based upon" credit, finding that the core of the short story was used in the film. The court wrote, "We think that King would have cause to complain if he were *not* afforded the 'based upon' credit." *Id.* at 831.

This case indicates the value of credits to the production company, which clearly thought it could sell more tickets by more closely linking Stephen King to the film. However, because King did not think well of the film, he preferred to limit his involvement rather than develop a reputation for producing films he deemed to be of low quality.

The possessory credit, which may be indicated as "a film by Hitchcock," "a Hitchock film," or "Hitchcock's *The Birds*," is rarely granted to writers. It is more often accorded to directors, such as D.W. Griffith or Cecil B. DeMille, who shape the final product from start to finish. Even so, the possessory credit can be controversial, given the number of contributors to the film.

In recent times, this credit appears more frequently on the big screen. One *Chicago Tribune* article said it has been "taken by any director whose agent can successfully negotiate for it." Marc Caro, *The Director or the Writer: Whose Film is It?*, CHICAGO TRIBUNE, Nov. 24, 2000. This *Chicago Tribune* article cites the possessor credit as appearing frequently on bombs, such as Bruce Paltrow's *Duets*, or even for a directorial debut, such as Sally Field's *Beautiful*.

Director David Lean makes the case for his possessory credit in relation to *Dr. Zhivago*:

> I worked one year with the writer. Unlike him [the writer], I directed not only the actors but the cameraman, set designer, costume designer, sound men, editor, composer and even the laboratory in their final print. Unlike him, I chose the actors, the technicians, the subject and him to write it. I staged it. I filmed it. It was my film of his script, which I shot when he was not there.

Id. Some directors, like Kevin Smith (*Clerks, Dogma, Jersey Girl*) refuse to take the "film by" credit. Smith said, "A film is probably the most collaborative art form there is.... No one person makes a movie. So taking that 'A film by' [credit] kind of leaves everybody out.... [This] means that there were no grips, there was no crew, there was no producer, [and] there was no PA production assistant that got the star to the set when you needed them." *Id.*

Producers have also sued to be accorded credit for their contributions to a film, as they are often the ones who find the initial project, secure the financing, and put the film together. For their efforts, the persons with the producer credit can win the Academy Award for Best Picture.

In *Tamarind Lithography Workshop v. Sanders*, Terry Sanders asserted that he acted as writer, director and a production manager by personally hiring and supervising personnel comprising the film crew for the film *Four Stones for Kanemitsu*, yet when the film screened at Tamarind's 10th anniversary celebration, it lacked the screen credit "A Film by Terry Sanders." Tamarind Lithography Workshop, Inc. v. Sanders, 143 Cal. App. 3d 571, 193 Cal. Rptr. 409 (Cal. Ct. App. 1983). At trial, the jury awarded Sanders $25,000, which was not contested on appeal. The California Appeals Court, however, expressed concerned as to whether this award could compensate "Sanders not only for past or preexisting injuries, but also for future injury (or injuries) as well." *Id.* at 574.

The court noted that the value of a film that is "favorably received by its critics and the public at large, can result in valuable advertising or publicity for the artists responsible for that film's making. Likewise, it is unquestionable that the nonappearance of an artist's name or likeness in the form of screen credit on a successful film can result in a loss of that valuable publicity. 'By its very nature, public acclaim is unique and very difficult, if not sometimes impossible, to quantify in monetary terms'." *Id.* at 576.

The court concluded that "pecuniary compensation for Sander's future harm is not a fully adequate remedy." It reversed the judgment denying Sander's request for injunctive relief to have his name added to the screen credits. *Id.* at 577, 579. In footnote 6 of the opinion, the court quoted three experts who opined in the 1983 case that the "a film by" credit for documentaries could be worth between $50,000 and $150,000. *Id.* at 577.

2. TELEVISION CREDITS

Similar to the film industry, a person's billing position in a television project determines his importance to the project and affects his future compensation. In *Smithers v. MGM Studios*, William Smithers sued MGM for breach of contract for failure to honor his "Most-Favored-Nations" billing arrangement. 139 Cal. App. 3d 643. 189 Cal. Rptr. 20, 22 (Cal. Ct. App. 1983). This provision read:

> "Except for the parts of DON WALLING, HELEN WALLING, and HOWARD RUTLEDGE, this deal is on a Most Favored Nations basis, i.e., if any other performer receives greater compensation than Artist, Artist shall receive that compensation.
>
> Additionally, no other performer shall receive more prominent billing or a better billing provision than Artist (except with respect to where his name is placed in the crawl)."

Id. The billing provision was to offset Smithers' agreement to accept a lower than usual compensation rate. MGM said that it used this provision to "get some good people to work for reasonably low money and to not have to take up a great deal of space in the main titles." *Id.*

When the pilot was screened, "Smithers saw that there were *four* actors with 'up-front' billing, instead of the agreed upon three actors.... Ultimately, ten or eleven actors were given 'up-front' billing, while Smithers' end-of-the-show-name-only billing remained the same." *Id.* In September 1976, Smithers complained that his billing was not in conformity with his contract. In mid-December 1976, he was told that his role was to be written out of the series. MGM also tried to get Smithers to waive the clause, which he refused to do and instead sued MGM.

At the trial, the jury ruled in favor of Smithers and awarded him damages of $3 million on four counts finding that MGM had committed the tort of breach of duty of good faith and fair dealing, breached its contract, and perpetrated fraud. Smithers agreed to reduce the verdict to $1,800,001 in return for denying MGM's motion for a new trial. On appeal, the judgment was affirmed. The Court of Appeals observed that there was sufficient evidence to support the jury's determination. On the fraud claim, for example, the Court of Appeals said the evidence indicated that MGM "had no intention of living up to its most-favored-nations provision, which was offered to induce Smithers to accept a lower than usual compensation rate."

This case alerts studios and producers that if they offer credit in lieu of compensation, they must live up to their agreement.

3. MUSIC CREDITS

In the music industry, musicians may fight over who is entitled to songwriter credit and over who warrants the performance credit. Composers who contribute the music and/or the lyrics are typically entitled to receive the songwriter credit. In Mozart and Beethoven's era, composers receive glory, some compensation, and immortality. While current songwriters may receive a measure of glory, most importantly they receive mechanical and performance royalties, which can sometimes result in a lifelong income stream. As a result, songwriters often make more money than performers because they get paid not only every time the song is performed whether on a concert stage or on the radio, but also for each song that is sold.

Some producers and some singers may seek to add their names to the writing credit as a means of receiving some of the royalties. The bigger the producer or singer, the more they can bargain for or even demand this credit. Producers who are known for crafting hit after hit, by bringing together the right back-up musicians and sound crew have more power.

However, songwriters with little clout may sometimes be left out of the credits and have to sue to have their names added.

In *Goodman v. Lee,* Shirley Goodman claimed that she co-wrote "Let the Good Times Roll' with Leonard Lee and sought to have the copyright registration changed to reflect her co-authorship.   815 F.2d 1030 (5th Cir. 1987). Goodman and Lee grew up in the same neighborhood and began composing songs together in 1952. The singers who recorded the 1956 "Let the Good Times Roll" included Barbara Streisand, Ray Charles, Roy Orbinson, and Jerry Lee Lewis. They made it Goodman & Lee's biggest hit.

Lee, who was responsible for their business affairs, registered the copyright in their early songs in both their names, but he registered later songs, including "Let The Good Times Roll," in his name alone. Goodman received no publishing royalties for songs registered solely under Lee's name. *Id.* at 1031. As the court noted in a footnote, publishing companies typically pay royalties, usually around 50%, to the author listed on the copyright registration. *Id.* at 1031 n.1.

Goodman did not learn of the error until the original copyrights were up for renewal in 1984. When she sought to have the copyright office add her name, she was informed that only the proprietor of the copyright could change the name. She then sued, requesting the court to include her name as co-author with Lee and to order an accounting of the royalty income. While the district court granted summary judgment for Lee's family, the court of appeals reversed, finding that Goodman is entitled to a trial to prove her claim of co-authorship of the song. *Id.* at 1032.

The jury agreed with Goodman, and awarded her damages. After several post-trial hearings, the district court entered a final judgment declaring Goodman a joint owner of the copyright of "Let The Good Times Roll," ordering the Register of Copyrights to identify her as co-author and joint owner of the copyright registration, and awarding her one-half of royalties received by the Lees from 1976 to 1993, together with prejudgment interest. The Fifth Circuit affirmed, 78 F.3d 1007, 1009 (5th Cir. 1996), and the Supreme Court denied the Lee's request for an appeal, 519 U.S. 861 (1996).

In *C & C Entertainment v. Rios-Sanchez*, 208 F.Supp.2d 139 (D.Puerto Rico 2002), the court declared that "A co-authorship claimant bears the burden of establishing that each of the putative coauthors (1) made independently copyrightable contributions to the work; and (2) fully intended to become co-authors." *Id.* at 142. Further, the court noted that in *Edward B. Marks Music Corp. v. Jerry Vogel*, 140 F.2d 268 (4th Cir. 1944), "a lyricist and composer were found to be coauthors where the lyricist wrote the words for the song ('December and May'), intending that someone else would eventually compose the music for those particular words. *Id.*

This court made a point of noting that authors do not have to work in concert, or even know each other to become joint authors. Rather, "it is enough that they mean their contributions to be complementary in the sense that they are to be embodied in a single work to be performed as such." *Id.*

Performance credits are listed on the album, CD, or cassette. Both the cover and the actual item will list the name of the group or individuals who performed the song(s). The group Milli Vanilli, composed of Rob Pilatus and Fabrice Morvan, was credited with the 1989 hit "Girl You Know It's True," which sold seven million copies in the U.S. and 30 million singles internationally. In 1990, Milli Vanilli won the Grammy award for Best New Artist.

While performing a concert, the sound system broke but the duo didn't realize it and continued to mouth the lyrics, exposing to the world that Milli Vanilli was a fraud created by German producer Frank Farian. Pilatus and Morvan were merely the public face for a group of anonymous musicians that included female singer Gina Mohammed and several other male singers including Charles Shaw, Johnny Davis, and Brad Howell. After the truth was revealed, Milli Vanilli became the first group ever stripped of a Grammy Award.

In *Freedman v. Arista Records*, several buyers sued in federal district court, charging Arista Records with fraud, misrepresentation and breach of warranty for promoting Milli Vanilli. 137 F. R. D. 225 (E.D. Pa. 1991). The plaintiffs sought certification of a clause to include all US purchasers of Milli Vanilli recordings prior to November 15, 1990. The plaintiffs argued that seven million people purchased the album because they believed Pilatus and Morvan personally sang the songs contained in the album.

The district court refused to certify the class, finding that the motion could not be granted under Rule 23 (b)(3), which requires class issues predominate over the individual ones. The court stressed the individualized reasons for purchasing music. The court observed:

> "What causes a person to respond positively to a performance is a complex matter, especially in these modern times where popular musical performances involve visual as well as auditory stimulation. One's response to art is personal and as such it is not susceptible to a class based determination of inducement."

While Arista won the lawsuit, the Milli Vanilli band disbanded. Pilatus and Morvan formed another group, called Rob & Fab, to prove they could really sing, but their debut sold only 2000 copies. Pilatus committed suicide in April 1998. Steve Huey, *Milli Vanilli*, *available at* http://www.allmusic.com/cg/amg.dll.

Milli Vanilli's downfall revealed an open secret about live concerts. Many fans often wonder while listening to a performance, "Is it live, or is it Memorex?" Lip-synching rumors have plagued musicians as diverse as Brittany Spears, Madonna, and Janet Jackson. Nevertheless, since they are mouthing the words to their own voices, these musicians do not create the performance credit problems of a Milli Vanilli.

B. COMPENSATION

As the discussion above has demonstrated, credit and billing are intricately linked to compensation. As noted in the *Smithers* case, actors will trade pay for credit to appear in a film that could help their careers. While unions negotiate the minimum compensation due talent in the film and television industries, the American Music Federation primarily assists musicians who are employed under collective bargaining arrangements, such as symphony orchestras. The AMF also offers sample contracts to aid bands and solo artists in negotiating their own compensation.

Much publicity is given to film actors, like Tom Hanks and Tom Cruse, who make upwards of $22 million a picture. They have hit the lottery, as the average compensation in the business is in the five-figure range. Similarly the television stars who make $1 million or more an episode are rare.

That said, film stars have been known to trade compensation for credit by appearing in lower budget films that showcase their talent in other genres. By augmenting their acting range, stars may receive a higher quality choice of scripts. After getting his start in sexually explicit films (*The Italian Stallion*) and then becoming known for action flicks (*Rocky*, *Rambo*, and *Cliffhanger*), which earned him as much as $20 million per picture, Sylvester Stallone received union negotiated scale wages to play a chubby, passive sheriff driven to action in a New Jersey town full of rogue New York cops in *Copland*. That film offered Stallone the opportunity to prove he could act alongside luminaries such as Academy Award winner Robert De Niro.

Above the title actors, such as Jim Carrey and Robin Williams who make $22 million a picture, have their compensation based on a cut of the box office gross receipts. Jack Nicholson, for example, received total compensation exceeding $56 million for playing the role of The Joker in the 1989 Batman, which was far more than one million dollars Michael Keaton earned for playing the title role.

The pay of stars often increases with the box office gross of their pictures. Bruce Willis, for example was paid $20 million for the 1995 *Die Hard with a Vengeance*, an increase by four times what he received for the original 1988 *Die Hard*. The former took in $365 million in worldwide box office compared to $139 million for the original film. In between, Willis starred in *Die Hard 2: Die Harder*, which earned $237,500,000. The increasing successes of these ventures enabled Willis to command higher fees.

Because the different components of the entertainment industry compensate their members in a variety of ways, this chapter will provide an overview of some of the differences in compensation by industry.

1. FILM & TELEVISION COMPENSATION

Two aspects of compensation that are peculiar to the film and television industries are "pay or play" and net compensation. Both issues are discussed in detail below.

a.   Pay or Play

Actors with considerable clout and who are in demand negotiate to include "pay or play" provisions in their contracts. If for any reason the project is cancelled, these clauses require producers or studios to compensate the artists or provide a comparable substitute.   These clauses recognize that actors turn down roles in order to accept a producer's or studio's project. The following is a "pay or play" provision from an international contract:

This Agreement is on a "pay or play" basis (as this term is understood in the UK film industry) PROVIDED THAT:

...the financier(s) providing the majority of the funding for the Film and the completion guarantor bonding the Film shall have gone on risk in relation to the Film, i.e. become so legally obligated without unfulfilled conditions precedent, within 3 weeks of the date hereof:

...the Artist shall mitigate the Producer's liability under this pay or play provision, whereby the liability hereunder shall be reduced to the extent that the Artist be remunerated for any services rendered to any third party during any period that would or could have constituted any part of the Rehearsal Period and/or the Shooting Period.[27]

This clause states the obligations of the producer to kick in once the financing is secure and an insurance company has guaranteed the film. Note also that the clause obligates the artist to look for work should the provision kick in. The actor is not permitted to sit around and wait for work, but rather he should actively seek to find other work.

---

[27] Reprinted with permission from Marc Vlessing, of Trendraise Company Limited.

In 1970, Academy Award-winning actress Shirley MacLaine litigated the true meaning of this provision. She sued Twentieth Century-Fox Film Corp. when it cancelled the musical "Bloomer Girl" and offered her a western "Big Country, Big Man" in its place. While the compensation was to remain at $750,000, MacLaine argued that the two were not the equivalent as required by her contract. "Bloomer Girl" would allow her to employ her song and dance talents and would be filmed in Los Angeles, whereas "Big Country, Big Man" was a straight dramatic role to be filmed in Australia. The new contract also eliminated her right to approve the director of the film and the screenwriter. The court agreed that the two films were not equivalent, and thus MacLaine was entitled to receive the $750,000 even though she had rejected the substitute film.

In an interview, MacLaine said that she "had turned down a year and a half of pictures to do 'Bloomer Girl'." She advises talent to "get the contract down and get it signed by everyone involved."[28] Neither "Bloomer Girl," which had opened October 5, 1944, at the Shubert Theatre and ran for 654 performances on Broadway, nor "Big Country, Big Man" were ever made into feature films.

Actress Raquel Welch sued MGM after it fired her from her starring role in the film *Cannery Row*. A jury found that MGM had

---

[28] *See* Burr & Henslee, *supra* note 1, at 258.

breached its contract, which contained a "pay or play clause," and ordered MGM to pay $2 million in compensatory damages and over $8 million in punitive damages. In affirming, the court of appeals noted that Welch was harmed by the loss of revenue from the additional film roles she would have obtained but for the firing and from loss of reputation. Raquel Welch v. MGM, 207 Cal.App.3d 164, 254 Cal. Rptr. 654, 663 (Cal. Sup. Ct. 1988).

Actress Cicely Tyson sued Elizabeth Taylor and her production company for violating the "pay or play" provision of her theatrical contract. Tyson agreed to play the lead role in the Broadway production of "The Corn is Green," which was to be taped for television. She was to receive $750,000 in a "pay or play guarantee," which reflected that Tyson, at the height of her career, would have to turn down other film, television, and stage opportunities to commit a year to "The Corn is Green." After a short run, the play was cancelled and never filmed for television. Regardless, the court found that Taylor and her production company owed Tyson the balance on her contract. *This is Me. Inc. v. Taylor*, 157 F.3d 139 (2nd Cir. 1998).

b. Net Compensation

Film and television artists often receive three types of compensation: guaranteed, deferred, and contingent. The first two are fairly easy to calculate and talent knows when they have not been paid. Contingent compensation can be based on gross or net revenues.

Gross compensation is paid based on the revenue generated at the box office. An actor who has contracted for gross participation points will receive a percentage of all box office and other revenues. Net compensation is paid after a number of subtractions, which leave the film or television show in a negative balance. Actors, writers, and other talent, who have contracted to receive net participation points, rarely receive additional compensation beyond guaranteed and deferred payments.

For example, Leonardo DiCaprio earned $1.8 million plus 18% of net compensation to star in *Titanic*, which earned $600,000,000 domestically as part of a global box office of around $2 billion. Like all movies, *Titanic* never earned a profit because of the studio's accounting system. DiCaprio received guaranteed compensation of $20,000,000 for his next picture *The Man in the Iron Mask*, which was released in 1998 and earned $57, million in the U.S., $126 million globally, for a total of $183 million. *See* Movie Box Office Figures, *available at* http://www.ldsfilm.com-/box/box.html.

On August 31, 1992, The Hollywood Reporter published an accounting of the picture *Rain Man*, which earned $228,112,545 as of May 31, 1992. The studio subtracted distribution fees, distribution expenses, and gross participation payouts, which left a balance of $16,582,814. Only then did it subtract $45,870,506 in production costs, which included direct costs, an overhead charge representing 15% of the production budget, and interest. The result was that *Rain Man* was in the hole.

Box office revenue	$222,112,545
-Distribution Fee	$ 79, 330,738
-Distribution Expenses	$ 54, 649,361
-Gross Participation Payouts	$ 77, 549,632
=Preliminary Balance	*$ 16, 582,814*
-Direct Production costs	$ 29, 098,523
-Overhead Charge (15%)	$ 4, 364,779
-Interest	$ 12, 407,204
=Final Balance	**($29,287,692)**

Those people expecting net profit payouts on a picture that cost $29 million to make, yet earned $228,112,546 at the box office, were out of luck.

Net profits are also referred to as backend profits. In an interview, screenwriter Walon Green said, "To obtain backend profits on my projects, I'd have to hire a forensic accountant. The cost of hiring the accountant and an attorney would probably exceed what the accountant found."[29] Art Buchwald discovered the truth of this statement the hard way.

Once Buchwald and his co-plaintiff Alain Bernheim won their initial lawsuit to have

---

[29] Burr & Henslee, *supra* note 1, at 19.

Buchwald credited with providing the idea for *Coming to America* and Bernheim as its producer, they found themselves in the uncomfortable position of having to enforce a contract that was based on net profits. In the second phase of the case, Judge Schneider found Paramount's definition of net profits unconscionable. Art Buchwald v. Paramount Pictures Corp., Second Phase, No. C706083 (Cal. Superior. Ct. Dec. 21, 1990).

Judge Schneider declared that following seven provisions of Paramount's net profit formula were unconscionable: (1) the 15% overhead on Eddie Murphy Productions Operational Allowance, (2) 10% advertising overhead not in proportion to actual cost, (3) 15% overhead not in proportion to actual costs, (4) charging interest on negative cost balance without credit for distribution fees; (5) chagrining interest on overhead; (6) charging interest on profit participation payments; (7) charging an interest rate of 20% to 30 %, which was not in proportion to the actual cost of the funds. *Id.* Schneider considered many of these items to be double charges, not in relationship to actual costs, and a method of hiding huge profits. *Id.*

In the third phase of the trial, Buchwald, Bernheim, and their attorney found out that even when you win, you lose. The court awarded Buchwald compensation of $150,000 for his idea based on his entitlement to 1.5% of net profits and his partner Alain Bernheim

$750,000 based on his initial entitlement to a minimum of 17.5% (reduced from 40%) of net profits. Art Buchwald v. Paramount Pictures Corp., Third Phase, No. 706083 (Cal. Superior Ct. Mar. 16, 1992). To win this judgment, their attorney Pierce O'Donnell, a partner at the prestigious Kaye Scholer, Fierman, Hays, & Handler's Los Angeles office, ran up a $2.5 million legal bill and over $500,000 in costs to complete the three and one-half year case.

O'Donnell, a former Supreme Court clerk to Justice Byron White, had taken the case on a contingency fee arrangement that made Buchwald & Bernheim responsible only for the cost of the trial. In the end, O'Donnell and his team spent $3 million to reap a judgment of $900,000 for their clients. O'Donnell wrote the book *Fatal Subtraction: How Hollywood Really Does Business* (1992), detailing the inside story of *Buchwald v. Paramount Pictures*, in part to recoup some of his investment. O'Donnell left Kaye Scholer in 1996 to start his own firm, O'Donnell & Shaeffer LLP.

Net profit stories are a legend in Hollywood, and yet some continue to file lawsuits. Benjamin Melniker and Michael Uslan sued Warner Brothers after their 13% net profit deal on the *Batman* films, which earned over $1 billion in box office revenues, yielded no further compensation than their $1,100,000 in fixed and deferred fees. The court found that they were not coerced into signing a net profit deal. Melniker was a former MGM general counsel and senior executive and "knew all the tricks of the trade." *Batfilm Productions, Inc.* v. Warner Bros., No. BC 051653 and No. BC 051654 (Cal. Superior Ct. Mar. 14, 1994). Melniker and Uslan argued that their contract was unfair to them because Warner Brothers and others earned millions of dollars on Batman and they did not. The court found this argument irrelevant, determining that while the contract may have been unfair, it was not unconscionable. *Id.*

Matt Damon and Ben Affleck, the writers and stars of the 1997 *Good Will Hunting*, found themselves in a position similar to the producers of *Batman.* Harvey Weinstein had invested between $15 and $20 million on *Good Will Hunting*, which returned a worldwide box office gross of $226 million, excluding network, cable, and video. Damon was paid an acting fee of $650,000, while Affleck received a little less. Weinstein eventually gave them a bonus of $500,000 each. In an interview with Peter Biskind, Affleck said, "*Good Will Hunting* had done enormously well by then, but we had gotten an accounting statement that said the movie was $50 million in the red.... You had to have some great accounting to hide net profits on that movie."[30]

Affleck further indicated that he and Damon had made a Faustian bargain with Weinstein

---

[30] Peter Biskind, Down And Dirty Pictures (2004), reprinted in VANITY FAIR, Feb. 2004, at 118, 166.

and his brother. "The exchange is," he said, "they'll spend money promoting the movie, they'll spend money on an Academy campaign, they'll win you an Oscar, and their reputation is they make better movies. But they're a nightmare to work with . . . So, yeah, we kind of got screwed, but when it came right down to it, it worked out great for us." Affleck also said that it worked out for them because he and Damon became highly paid actors, able to command $10 - $20 million per picture. *Id.*

Television writers, actors, directors, and producers experience the same problems trying to collect net profits on their hits. Anthony Yerkovich sued MCA and Universal for net compensation due him for writing the pilot teleplay that Universal subsequently produced as *Miami Vice.* Yerkovich v. MCA, 11 F.Supp.2d 1167 (C.D. Cal. 1997). The court of appeals affirmed the district court's finding that even if it accepted Yerkovich's interpretation of his agreement, there was insufficient admissible evidence showing that he was entitled to additional money. Yerkovich v. MCA, 2000 WL 234591 (9th Cir. 2000). The Supreme Court denied his petition for a writ of certiorari.

B.   MUSIC COMPENSATION

Musicians may earn money from composing songs, from tour performances, from merchandizing their group name, and from royalties on their records. Successful musicians, like Michael Jackson, have been known to amass million dollar empires at the height of their careers. In a 2003 television interview, Jackson claimed to be worth over a billion dollars.

Symphony conductors with top orchestras are among the more highly paid musicians who receive salaries for their services. The New York Times revealed on July 4, 2004, that the New York Philharmonic paid Lorin Maazel $2,280,000 during the 2002-03 concert year and the Chicago Symphony paid Daniel Barenboim $2,140,000 during the 2001-02 concert year. The Times reported that "[a]mong the18 American orchestras with 52-week contracts, at least seven pay their music directors more than $1 million, and three pay their manger more than $700,000. Blair Tindal, *The Plight of the White-Tie Worker*, N.Y. TIMES, July 4, 2004, at Sec. 2, p. 1. The Times also stated, "[A]s pay increases for symphony leaders soared, the player's annual raises dropped from 3.9 percent in 1993 to 1.7 percent in 2003." *Id.* at 24.

Early in their careers, musicians write and perform in other genres often find themselves in positions similar to beginning film and television stars whereby they accept bad deals in order to get their records made. Composers, as discussed above, receive royalties based on their copyright credits. Performers may receive a flat fee, a percentage of the box office revenues, or a combination thereof depending on how big they are. Merchandizing revenue stems from trademarking the musician's or band's name and then applying it to products ranging from t-shirts and posters to programs and any other memorabilia that resonates with fans.

It is the record contracts that give musicians the most heartache, causing them to bargain for as much upfront payment as possible. The royalty payments, representing a percent of the sales revenue, often shock musicians when they receive their statements, particularly if they have produced a gold or platinum album and spent money in anticipation of a big payout. The problem is similar to the net profit scenario in film & television in that the key factor is to determine what is subtracted from gross revenues.

The contract may subtract recording cost, advances to producers and musicians, video production cost, excess mechanicals, royalties payable to the producer, packaging costs, promotional, and a percent for reserves against returns before paying any royalty to the musicians. This royalty rate decreases on mid-price and budget records by as much as 50%, although Peter Thall says that the rate can be increased to a two-thirds rate for budget records and a three-quarters rate for mid-price records. Thall, *supra* note 13, at 28. Thall says that the royalty rate may also be reduced for singles, for foreign sales, and for record clubs. *Id.* at 28-29. Even when the record companies support the cost of tours, they deduct any money advanced from the royalties. *Id.* at 33. All these deductions can leave the musicians owing their recording company money or waiting for payments that may never arrive.

CHAPTER 8

ENTERTAINMENT CONTRACTS

William Shakespeare's plays are in the public domain, which means any film, television, or theater company may reproduce or perform them without acquiring a contract, paying fees or seeking permission. If, however, an entertainment company wants to perform a play that is protected by copyright or acquire an actor, author, director, or other personnel, the company must seek permission, which is manifested in a contract.

All contracts in the entertainment industry must contain answers to the classic questions of who, what, when, where and how much. Contracts may be oral or written, implied or expressed. The contractual terms should serve to guide the parties in their business interactions.

Written contracts endeavor to spell out precisely what is expected of the parties involved. Oral contracts are also a staple of the industry. Personal service contracts have always raised problems, particularly the question of when to hold someone to a contract may be when to hold someone to a contract may be considered as running afoul of the 13th Amendment to the Constitution, which prohibits slavery. Nevertheless, entertainers do back out of deals. Sometimes, they are better off honoring a commitment than wincing on a deal, as they may be sued and forced to pay tremendous damages if someone has relied on their commitment.

Some entertainers discover, to their detriment, that they are bound by their oral agreements once another party has acted to secure financing based on the expectation that actors' words are their bonds.

A.   **FILM CONTRACTS**

Whether oral or written, it is important for talent to understand the provisions of their contracts before they sign them. *Main Line Pictures v. Basinger*, 1994 WL 814224 (Cal. Ct. App. 1994), involved three types of contracts: an oral agreement, a deal memo, and a long-form agreement. In that case, the question became whether actress Kim Basinger had indeed contractually committed to star in the film *Boxing Helena.* After the trial evidence was presented, the jury concluded that Basinger and/or Mighty Wind, her loan-out corporation, had entered into oral and written agreements that they breached.

The California Court of Appeals observed that the jury found direct evidence that

Basinger herself entered into a contract with Main Line. There was testimony that she personally discussed the project with her attorney, and she gave her agents the authority to bind her in the contract. The documents referred to Basinger's performance. Further, there was the evidence to support the contention that Mighty Wind entered into the contract with Main Line. The discussions took place at Mighty Wind's offices. There was also a written agreement between Mighty Wind and Basinger and the deal memos evidenced a contract with Mighty Wind. Basinger was ultimately held responsible for having breached a contract with Main Line Pictures.

In addition to the truism that entertainers are bound by their contracts, they must also be aware of standard practices that are inferred into contracts. Director Otto Preminger, for example, admitted that when he signed the agreement to have *Anatomy of a Murder* shown on television, he was aware that the practice in the television industry was to interrupt motion pictures for commercials and to make minor cuts. Although he was aware of the practice, the court found in *Preminger v. Columbia* Pictures, 49 Misc. 2d 363, 267 N.Y.S. 2d 594 (S.Ct. 1966), that Preminger did not specifically negotiate to change conditions prevalent in the industry. Industry practices may be altered, but they must be done so expressly in a written agreement.

Insurance contracts are also important to filmmaking as they guarantee that the picture will be completed. Problems arise when actors die, such as when the singer Aaliyah tragically perished in a plane crash before completing her role in *The Matrix: Reloaded.* Nona Gaye, the daughter of singer Marvin Gaye, replaced Aaliyah.

In *CNA Intern. Reinsurance Co. Ltd. v. Phoenix*, 678 So. 2d 373 (Fla. App. 1 Dist. 1996), an insurance company sued an actor's estate to recover their payments to their insured. At the time actor River Phoenix died after taking an overdose of drugs, he was committed to star in two films, *Dark Blood* and *Interview with the Vampire.* After Phoenix's death, *Dark Blood* was abandoned and *Interview with the Vampire* was completed with actor Christian Slater replacing Phoenix.

The insurance companies sued his estate for breach of contract, alleging that Phoenix was "under a general obligation not to do anything that would deprive the parties to the agreement of its benefits." CNA argued that "by deliberately taking illegal drugs in quantities in excess of those necessary to kill a human being, Phoenix deprived the parties of his services and breached his obligation." *Id.* CNA also charged that Phoenix had signed a fraudulent medical certificate in which he denied having ever used "LSD, heroin, cocaine, alcohol in excess, or any other narcotics, depressants, stimulants or other narcotics, depressants, stimulants or psychedelics whether prescribed or not prescribed by a physician." *Id.*

After the trial court dismissed the action with prejudice, finding that death excused performance of the contract, the Florida District Court of Appeal affirmed. It determined that "the parties to the agreements could have provided specifically for the contingent of loss due to the use of illegal drugs, as they provided for other hazardous or life threatening conditions." *Id.*

Insurance companies consider actors like Robert Downey Jr., who has been imprisoned for drug and alcohol problems, to be a high risk and increase rates accordingly. If the rates rise significantly or an actor becomes uninsurable, production companies and studios may forgo working with that actor. According to the *New York Times*, Downey was set to star in a Woody Allen project when producers dropped him after they "found out that there was no affordable way to resolve the cost of insuring him." Mim Udovitch, The Sobering Life of Robert Downey Jr., N.Y. TIMES MAG, Oct. 19, 2003, at 35.

2. TALENT CONTRACTS

a. Actors Contracts

During her trial, Kim Bassinger was asked under direct examination, "At what time can you breach an agreement?" She answered,

"Anytime I want to." Burr and Henslee, supra note 1, at 180.

Ms. Basinger found out the hard way that contracts must be obeyed when the jury awarded a verdict of $9.8 million to the Main Line Pictures, which was double their request. Unable to pay, Basinger declared bankruptcy and sold the town she had bought for $20 million for $1 billion.

Actors give both oral consent and sign contracts to procure their services. Such contracts will state the term of the engagement (the number of weeks for rehearsals and principal photography); the remuneration (how much the actor is to be paid and in what installments); expense payments (for transportation, housing and per diem); and the actress's services and obligations (specifying that the actress will complete the role and comply with all directions). A health provision requires the actress to indicate that she is not suffering from any physical or mental incapacity that would prevent her from rendering services. Other provisions may deal with copyright, dubbing, insurance, and force majeure. If the actress becomes incapacitated or fails to perform her services, the producer may suspend her services.

Shirley MacLaine, who has been acting for 50 years, advises her colleagues to "get the contract down and get it signed by everyone involved.... [W]hatever is in the contract should be observed." Burr and Henslee, *supra* note 1, at 258.

b. Writer Contracts

Author Tony Hillerman advises writers that when they receive Hollywood option money, "Tear open the envelope and run out and cash the check immediately. The writer's role in movies is to listen and nod." Burr and Henslee, *supra* note 1, at 414.

Writers like Hillerman provide source material to Hollywood production companies. A producer will ask the author of a printed novel to sign an option agreement, which gives the producer a specified time period to pull together all the major components of the project—script, actors, directors, financing, and crew. With the option contract, the writer gives film rights in return for credit (usually a "based upon" credit) and a fee, but he retains the remainder of the copyright unless the contract says otherwise.

Hillerman told the author of this book about an incident early on when he accidentally gave up the rights to "Joe Leaphorn," his principal protagonist. His option contract said that when the final payment was made, the producer would own all rights to the book. Hillerman had to retain an attorney to retrieve the rights to his character.

Screenwriters use books like Hillerman's *A Thief of Time* and *Skinwalkers* to turn them into scripts for television or feature films. Screenwriters may also generate original material of their own. Screenwriters may be engaged for a particular period of time to pen a script, with delivery periods established to indicate when the drafts, re-writes and the polish draft are due. The writer may receive sole or shared screenplay credit depending on how much of his words make it into the final draft. If there are several writers, the Writers Guild may arbitrate to determine who is entitled to credit.

The screenwriter's contract will also state the upfront compensation, which is set to delivery of material, payments for additional services, bonus, and deferred or contingent compensation. Some screenwriters' contracts attempt to tie the author in advance to a sequel. The screenwriters' contract may also set performance standards, requiring prompt, diligent and conscientious effort and state the circumstances under which the screenwriter may be terminated. These contracts frequently state the producers' ownership rights, and that these rights can be assigned.

While writers should read their contracts in advance, too often they don't and are later surprised. Walon Green says some writers don't give their contracts to a lawyer "and they end up in trouble. They wait to find a lawyer when they haven't been paid. By then it may be too late." Burr and Henslee, *supra* note 1, at 19.

c. Director Contracts

Stephen Frears, who directed *Dangerous liaisons* and *Dirty Pretty Things*, advises creators involved in the business not to "take any money until they are sure they want to work with particular people." Frears was once sued by a producer after he orally agreed to do a film and the producer sent his agent some money before he had a chance to review the script. He says, "When I saw the script I realized it wasn't for me and I decided to back out." Burr and Henslee, *supra* note 1, at 109. Frears says he learned, "Taking money creates a contract and expectations that you are really going to do the picture."

A contract to engage a director's service will specify the working title of the motion picture, the term of the engagement and the services. These contracts divide the time period by pre-production (meetings, location searches, and rehearsals) production (principal photography, and post-production (editing, cutting, and final mix). The compensation is divided into fixed, allocated in connections to the production periods, deferred amounts, and contingent or net compensation.

Directors of a certain stature may have a "pay or play" provision, obligating the production company to pay the director or offer an alternate film if the one under contract falls through. These contracts specify the living, transportation, and other expenses to which the director is entitled to be allocated in advance or reimbursed.

The director may also be held to certain specified performance standards, which permit the production company to fire the director if he does not live up to them or becomes incapacitated. The director may have to warrant that they are not under any current disabilities or agreements that would affect his or her participation on the picture. With warranties come indemnities, requiring the director to compensate or reimburse the production company if the director breaches his guarantees.

Perhaps the most important advice for directors comes from Stephen Frears. He says he now makes certain that he wants to work with "the particular people and their picture" before he takes money and/or signs a contracts. *Id.*

B. TELEVISION CONTRACTS

Contracts are important to every aspect of television production, from the idea stage to the final exhibition and licensing of material for distribution on videotapes or DVDs. As in film, TV contracts may be oral or written. If oral, the question becomes whether there was sufficient agreement among the parties to form a contract. Even when there are written pages available, the parties must clearly intend their words to form a contract.

The plaintiff in *Panizza v. Mattel*, 2003 WL 22251317 (S.D.N.Y. 2003), confronted the issue of how to enforce the use of an idea without an express contract. Like film plaintiffs before her, Panizza sought to have the law imply a quasi contract because she gave the ideas in confidence. In doing so, she found herself in a bind once the defendants removed the case to federal court, which requires a federal question when the two parties are from the same jurisdiction. She properly brought the idea case in state court, but once it was removed to federal jurisdiction, she would have been better served if she had alleged copyright infringement as a first issue.   She proved once again the difficulty of bringing an idea case based on quasi contract theory.

Letters may also form the basis of a contract, if the parties manifested sufficient intent that they do so. In *Burr v. American National Theatre and Academy*, 103 N.Y.S.2d 589 (N.Y. Sup. Ct. 1951), Eugene Burr sued the defendants for breach of contract based on letters dated May 15, 1950. He alleged that the defendants had committed to pay him and his partner $1000 per show if they procured a sponsor. The court found that the plaintiffs had performed their duties but the defendants had not; therefore, it reversed the prior dismissal of the action.

Even when the contracts spell out precisely the obligation of all parties, disputes can arise as to whether they have been carried out. Sanda Fulton Gabriel sued ABC for violating their contract to compensate her if they turned her idea and pilot for a talk show called *Girl Friends* into a full-fledged production. Girl Friends Productions v. ABC, 2000 WL1505978 (S.D.N.Y. 2000). When *The View* premiered in August 1997, Gabriel thought they had done so. ABC maintained that *The View*, which featured Barbara Walters and four other female hosts of varying ages was created and produced by Walter's Barwall Productions, Inc. The court agreed and granted summary judgment to ABC. It did not find any substantial similarity between the two shows.

The terms of the contract may create a clash if one party argues that it gave them a right that the other party disputes. In *Wexley v. KTTV*, the sole issue was whether the 1931 contract gave the purchaser the right to televise a motion picture. 108 F.Supp. 558 (S.D.Cal. 1952). The third clause of the contract granted the purchaser "complete, entire, and exclusive motion picture rights in and to the said dramatic compositions." The court determined that the clause granted the right to televise motion pictures, "unless a limitation or reservation is expressly and clearly imposed." *Id.* at 559.

In this contract, Clause C reserved for the plaintiff "television rights unaccompanied by a visual representation of the play." The plaintiff contended that "a motion picture is not a visual representation of the play" but the court disagreed. While the uses of television in 1951 may not have been foreseeable in 1931, the parties did contemplate and convey television rights. A 15-year restriction was applied to "live television" only because it was considered the most serious competition to the exhibition of motion pictures, but they did not restrict all television. *Id.* at 560. The court granted judgment for the defendants.

Another important aspect of television contracts is that no party can give away more rights than he has. Gilliam v. ABC, 538 F.2d 14 (2nd Cir. 1976), involved a series of contracts between several parties. The British Broadcasting Corporation (BBC) contracted with the Monty Python group to require them to write and deliver 30-minute scripts for use in a televisions series. While BBC retained final authority to make changes to the scripts, only minor changes could be made without prior consultation with the writers. Nothing in the agreement permitted BBC to alter a recorded program.

BBC did have permission to license the programs to be shown in overseas territories. It contracted with Time-Life Films to distribute the Monty Python shows in the United States. BBC gave Time-Life the rights to edit the programs for insertion of commercials, applicable censorship or governmental rules and regulations, although BBC did not have such rights in its own agreements with the Monty Python group.

Time Life Films then sold to ABC the right to broadcast excerpts from various Monty Python programs. Monty Python objected to ABC's plans to broadcast two 90-minute specials comprised of three 30-minute Monty Python programs. Of the 90 minutes, ABC had eliminated 24 minutes to devote to commercials. When Monty Python saw the first special, they were " 'appalled' at the discontinuity and 'mutilation' that had resulted from the editing done by Time-Life for ABC." *Id.* at 18. They sought an injunction to keep ABC from broadcasting the second special.

The judge granted their request for an injunction, finding they would suffer harm to their reputation that would be irreparable from the showing of the special. The judge said, "ABC may obtain no solace form the fact that editing was permitted in the agreements between BBC and Time-Life or Time-Life and ABC." *Id.* at 21. Further, he noted, " BBC was not entitled to make unilateral changes in the script and was not specifically empowered to alter the recordings once made." *Id.* Since Monty Python had reserved all rights not granted to the BBC to itself, BBC's contract to allow Time-Life, and the latter's subsequent contract with ABC, to permit editing was a nullity. The court agreed that ABC had distorted Monty Python's work.

Perhaps because the Monty Python group was from a foreign country, the court did not infer into their contract with BBC and between BBC and Time-Life knowledge about the industry. In two prior cases, courts held that when the film artists authorized a television showing of their work, they were bound by industry standards that permitted a right to edit and cut for television. *See* Preminger v. Columbia Pictures, 49 Misc. 2d 363, 267 N.Y.S.2d 594 (Sup. Ct. 1966), and Autry v. Republic Productions, 213 F.2d 667 (9th Cir. 1954). Possibly, the difference is that editing for commercials was not the industry standard in Britain at the time. When Monty Python granted BBC the right to license production overseas, they expected the British television standards to prevail.

C. MUSIC CONTRACTS

The music industry employs a variety of contracts from band partnership agreements, which set up the formation of the band and how it will run, to band/management agreements that establish the relationship between manager and the band, to band/agent agreements that set out the expectation of the band's booking agent. The contract that musical groups sign with their attorney establishes the attorney's duty to the band. Their agreements with songwriters and producers set up mutual obligations.

1. BAND & SYMPHONY AGREEMENTS

A key component of the band partnership agreement concerns the name and who acquires use of the name in the event that the band dissolves. In *Kassbaum v. Steppenwolf Productions, Inc.,* 236 F.3d 487 (9th Cir. 2000), Nicholas Kassbaum was sued for referring to himself as "formerly of Steppenwolf," an "original member of Steppenwolf," or an "original founding member of Steppenwolf." The court of appeals reversed the district court's grant of a permanent injunction to prohibit Kassbaum's use of the name.

Kassbaum conceded that his 1980 contract "absolutely precludes" him from "performing, sponsoring or endorsing a band entitled Steppenwolf." *Id.* at 491. In its review, the court of appeals considered that the ownership and control of the name was transferred from party to party through a series of contracts. It was the 1980 contract that "effected the transfer of the trade name Steppenwolf from Kassbaum and The New Steppenwolf to SPI and SI and led to Kassbaum's discontinuing to perform under 'The New Stepenwolf'." *Id.* at 492.

Nevertheless, the court considered too broad the contract clause permitting the band to use the name "for any purposes whatsoever." The court concluded that Kassbaum should be allowed to identify himself as a former member of the band as this was unlikely to create consumer confusion as the source of the band's music." *Id.* at 492-493.

Bands also have to be careful to not lose the use of their name. In *Far Out Productions, Inc. v. Oskar*, 247 F.3d 986 (9th Cir. 2001), a dispute arose over the use of the band name "War." Harold Brown, an original member of the group, filed a direct action against Far Out Productions, claiming that it obtained the trademark fraudulently. The district court disagreed and the court of appeals affirmed.

On April 1, 1987, Far Out Productions agreed in writing with each of the band members to reaffirm "Far Out Productions' exclusive ownership in the name 'War'." Thereafter, an incontestability affidavit was filed with the Patent and Trademark Office declaring that Far Out Productions owned the mark and that it had been in continuous use for five years. *Id.* at 990. The band lost its name through not understanding the full consequences of the contracts they signed.

The American Federation of Musicians negotiates symphony orchestra contracts on behalf of their members. Guillermo Figueroa, the conductor of the New Mexico Symphony Orchestra and an AFM member, says, "It was true that for a very long time that management was not favorable to players. With the advent of the unions, musicians have done much better." Burr and Henslee, *supra* note 1, at 661. As a consequence, symphony orchestras are governed by a master agreement negotiated for a term of years. Figueroa says the disadvantage of such an agreement is "[i]t's hard to change things once the agreement is done, even when common sense tells you that you can break something if it is in everyone's best interest. However, both sides feel that if they open up a certain point that is not in the contract, the other side will want something in return." *Id.*

Symphony orchestras are, however, better off than in the era of conductor Leonard Bernstein, who "was known to fire musicians on the spot if they played off key one too many times," says conductor Sam Wong. Wong adds, "Artur Rodzinski, a former conductor of the New York Philharmonic...was reported to have carried a loaded gun when he rehearsed. And, of course, people didn't cross his path." *Id.* at 660-661.

2. BAND-MANAGEMENT AGREEMENTS

The right manager can assist in developing a band's career and taking them to the next level. Managers with contacts in the music business can get the band recording contracts and the right contacts. Managers ideally seek musicians who are professional and committed to their music. Once band members become famous or superstars, the manager's role evolves.

One manager, who wished to remain anonymous, of a famous band said his challenges include dealing with band members who hate each other and no longer enjoy performing together. The band members have also been inflicted with publicly documented personal problems ranging from collapsing marriages to ongoing abuse of drugs and alcohol. This manager cites that one of his principal jobs is arranging for lawyers to address legal problems and staging interventions to encourage the band members to take action on their personal problems. This band, which wrote their own music and have had it constantly recorded by other musicians, generates an ongoing stream of income from their publishing royalties.

Musicians and their managers have been known to dispute entitlement to royalties. When conflict arises, the court reviews their contract. In *Ahern v. Scholz,* 85 F.3d 774 (1st Cir. 1996), a manager and a musician traded claims and counterclaims over which, one owed the other money for breaching their agreements. Donald Thomas Scholz, a musician, composer, and record producer with the group Boston, accused the manager Paul Ahern of failing to render direct accountings every six months and pay the appropriate royalties of $277,000 for a total of $459,000 with interest. While Ahern admitted at trial that he had failed to make some payments he owed Scholz, the jury did not consider his actions a material breach.

Ahern counterclaimed that Scholz owed him a share of the $6 million in royalties the third album earned from selling over 4 million copies. Scholz presented Ahern with an "Artist Royalty Statement," which, after deductions for a producer share and artists costs, fell to a net below zero. *Id.* at 782-783. Scholz maintained that he was excused from rendering an accounting to Ahern on the third album until Ahern had paid him on the first two albums. The court of appeals decided that Scholz was entitled to have this issue considered by a jury and remanded the case for further consideration.

This case illustrates the needs of both sides to keep on top of accounting issues. Both sides benefit when discrepancies are handled immediately rather than being permitted to fester and develop into further conflict.

Sometimes a disagreement can develop as to what is the nature of the manager's duties. Because managers are responsible for the band's overall career, their activities can sometimes overlap with those of agents. As their manager, Dave Park had a written contract to manage the Deftones in return for a 20 percent commission on all income earned from the employment he secured.

Park also procured 84 performance engagements and a recording contract for them with Maverick Records without being a licensed agent. Under the California Talent Agencies Act, these activities are by all individuals unless they are licensed as a talent agent. The court observed that the job of personal managers is "primarily advise, counsel, direct and coordinate the development of the artist career. They advise in both business and personal matters, frequently lend money to young artists and serve as spokespersons for the artists." Park v. Deftones, 41 Cal. App. 4th 1465, 1469-1470 (Cal. Ct. App. 1999). Because Park would receive a commission from obtaining the recording contract, he was in affect acting as an agent. The court affirmed the Labor Commissioner's decision to void the management agreements.

3. BAND-AGENT AGREEMENTS

Band agent agreements may similarly be voided if the agent fails to perform his or her duties in a customary fashion. Country singer Loretta Lynn's contract with the Wil-helm Agency required it to represent and advise her in the "radio, television, recording and personal appearances field" of the entertainment industry "throughout the world and in outer space for a period of [t]wenty years." The agency was obliged to procure employment, negotiate advertising and commercial tie-ups for using her name and likeness, and to counsel her on matters of professional interest. Wil-helm Agency v. Lynn, 618 S.W.2d 748 (Tenn. Ct. App. 1981).

This agreement was straight forward, but it required professional individuals to be properly implemented. Loretta Lynn initially worked closely with Teddy Wilburn who spent several hours almost daily with her, assisting her in rewriting songs and advising her on costumes, mannerisms, and lines. Loretta's career thrived during this period. Teddy Wilburn then left the firm after his brother Doyle began to consume excessive amounts of alcohol. Smiley Wilson then joined the firm and became Loretta's agent for a short while until Teddy was persuaded to return.   When Teddy left again, Doyle began acting as Loretta's agent.

Doyle committed several acts of misconduct that reflected poorly on Loretta. He insulted the producer of the Johnny Carson Show during negotiations for Loretta to appear on the show. He disturbed Loretta during performances. While drunk, he once vomited on a dinner table at a post-performance party given for patrons, promoters, disc jockeys and their wives. He displayed public drunkenness during the London tour, while Loretta was taping the Ed Sullivan Show, and during every road trip. After Loretta employed an attorney, he alerted the agency that they were in breach of their duties and she was no longer bound by the contract.

The court agreed that the agency was in breach, finding Doyle Wilburn's conduct "entirely inconsistent with the duty owed the artist under the contract." *Id.* at 751. The court noted that each party owed the other obligations under the bilateral contract and were required to "restrain from doing any act that would delay or prevent the other party's performance of the contract." *Id.* at 751-752.

4. BAND-ATTORNEY AGREEMENTS

Relationships with attorneys are similarly important for bands to establish. Attorneys possess ethical obligations to perform their agreements with their clients in a standard in accordance with the law.

In *Croce v. Kurnit*, the widow of Jim Croce sued his attorney for fraud and breach of contract and sought rescission of the contracts between Jim and the company that represented him. 565 F.Supp. 884 (S.D.N.Y. 1982). Attorney Phillip Kurnit served as an officer of the publishing and managerial companies that signed Croce to recording, publishing, and managerial contracts. Kurnit never advised Croce and his wife to obtain outside counsel prior to signing the agreements on September 17, 1968. In the fall of 1968, Kurnit represented the Croces in connection with a lease agreement and by April 1969 was listing his firm as the party to whom all business related correspondence for Croces should be sent. He also executed a document as attorney in fact for them and became involved in a dispute between them and their managers. *Id.* at 888.

When Croce wrote Kurnit seeking to terminate his contracts, Kurnit relayed their concerns to the management company. After Jim Croce perished in a plane crash in 1973,

Kurnit became the attorney for the estate. Later, Ingrid Croce sought another attorney to bring an action against Kurnit for breach of fiduciary duty.

The court found that in some instances, Kurnit did not act as their attorney, but nevertheless "a lawyer may owe a fiduciary obligation to persons with whom he deals," particularly when they have reason to believe they can rely on him. *Id.* at 890. Kurnit had introduced himself to the Croces as "the lawyer" and explained the "legal ramifications" of the contracts to them. *Id.* He should have advised them to obtain outside counsel. Because he did not, he breached a fiduciary duty to them. *Id.*

Notwithstanding Kurnit's actions, Ingrid Croce was unable to obtain rescission of the agreements as unconscionable. The court considered the contracts to be "hard bargains, signed by an artist without bargaining power, and favored the publishers, but as a matter of fact did not contain terms which shock the conscience or differed so grossly from industry norms as to be unconscionable by their terms." *Id.* at 898. Due to uncertainty in the music business and the high risk of failure for new performers, the court said, "the contracts, though favoring the defendants, were not unfair." *Id.* While the contracts could not be rescinded, Ingrid Croce was entitled to the damages that resulted from Kurnit's breach of fiduciary duty for failing to advise the Croces to seek independent counsel. *Id.* at 894.

The *Croce* case indicates the importance of creating a contract between lawyers and clients. It should then be clear to the lawyer to whom he owes a fiduciary duty. Lawyers should never represent both sides of a contract without advising the other side that they should obtain independent counsel. If the other side chooses to forge ahead, the lawyer should have them sign a statement that they have been cautioned to seek another lawyer and chose not to.

D. PUBLISHING CONTRACTS

Entertainers, who make their living in film, television, and music, often write books to tell their life stories or reveal their side of a major news event. Sometimes they write books themselves, but more often they are ghostwritten or heavily edited by the publishers. Others write books about entertainers.

Film actress Anne Heche wrote *Call Me Crazy* to discuss her various relationships with men and women and explain a well known episode where she acted bizarre while high on ecstasy. In her memoir, television star Rosanne Barr divulged that she suffered from a multiple personality disorder. Scholars and producers continue to find material in Wolfgang Amadeus Mozart's life over two hundred years after his death for their books and films.

Publishing contracts to produce articles and books range from simple one paragraph letters to complex documents. A contract to publish an article in a magazine can be as simple as the following letter agreement written to author Gregg Levoy[31] from *Vogue Magazine* on February 10, 1988:

> Dear Gregg,
> As discussed, this confirms your assignment for a piece on self-defense courses. The piece will be 1500 words in length and we will pay you $1250. It is due in mid-February. If it isn't published, I will pay you half that amount.

The "who" are the parties to the contract: Gregg Levoy and *Vogue Magazine.* The "what" is an assignment to write an article on self-defense courses. The "when" is the due date, by mid-February 1988. The "where" is left up to Levoy who just has to produce the piece. The "how much" is clearly stated in that *Vogue* will pay Levoy $1250 if they publish his piece and $625 if they kill the piece. More commonly, this is called a "kill fee," which pays the author for some of his or her time in researching and writing the article.

Notice that the letter was silent on the issue of copyright. When nothing is said, the author retains all rights to the copyright, with the exception of first publication rights that he granted the publisher. In a separate contract to

---

[31] The author thanks Gregg Levoy for providing this letter to be used in training law students.

write an article on third world debt for another major magazine, however, Mr. Levoy signed away these rights. The contract termed the relationship a "work made for hire," and noted that the magazine would retain the contract.

This two-page contract also required Levoy to warrant that (a) he was the sole author of the work; (b) the work is original and does not infringe the copyright of another person; and (c) the work has not been previously published. Levoy would be required to indemnify the magazine if he violated any of these warranties. The magazine also retained the right to edit or make other changes to his work.

Book contracts can also be as short as two pages or lengthy. Most will contain some version of the clauses discussed below.

1. MANUSCRIPT CLAUSE

Many book contracts begin with a standard clause dealing with the specifics of the manuscript: the title, the name of the author, the length, the due date, how many copies the author must deliver in hard copy and on disk. Sometimes, in this clause the publisher reserves the right to reject the final manuscript as unacceptable or un-publishable.

A savvy negotiator, such as television star Joan Collins' former attorney Swifty Lazar, may be able to get the publisher to waive this clause, but this is rare. Instead, authors may insert that the publisher's right of rejection must be "reasonably exercised," but this is often implied in the contract. Publishers rarely reject a manuscript at the final stages unless they think that it is justifiably un-publishable.

What makes a manuscript un-publishable? The final draft may not be as well written as the initial proposal, it may contain information the publisher deems libelous, or the subject of the book has become dated. Documentary filmmaker Michael Moore was scheduled to have HarperCollins publish his book *Stupid White Men* on September 11, 2001, the day that terrorists struck the World Trade Center. In a *60 Minutes* interview, he said that HarperCollins called him and said because the world has changed, he needed to change the title and re-write 50% of the book, removing the negative references to President Bush. *See* 60 Minutes (CBS Television Broadcast, June 27, 2004). Moore read pages from a book to a group, and a librarian present started an e-mail campaign. After receiving numerous e-mails from librarians throughout the country, HarperCollins released the book in the spring of 2003. *Id.*

The changing social climate that greeted Moore's book exemplifies why publishers insist on keeping an "out" clause in the contract. It permits them to cancel publication or request substantial changes to the book. If negotiations fail, they may return all rights to the author.

If a publisher does exercise its "out" clause or decides to "kill" the project, what happens to the author's advance? If the advance is tied to the production of an acceptable manuscript, and the publisher deems the author's book unacceptable, then the author must refund the advance. If the publisher kills the project for reasons that have nothing to do with the author's performance, the author has a strong case for keeping the funds. With magazine articles, contracts will specify the "kill fee" in advance, such as the one between *Vogue* and Gregg Levoy.

In one profile case, publisher HarperCollins sued actress/author Joan Collins for return of a substantial advance after she turned in a manuscript that it deemed un-publishable. A jury, however, decided that not only did she not have to return the advance even though HarperCollins found her manuscript unacceptable, but also that HarperCollins had to pay her part of the additional monies due on her contract. Ms. Collins won because instead of the usual manuscript clause requiring her to produce an acceptable manuscript, Ms. Collins' contract merely required her to produce a completed manuscript.

2. COPYRIGHT ISSUES

Depending on the type of publisher, the contract may require the publisher to register the copyright in the name of the author or in the name of the publisher. Most of the big publishing companies that sell to the publisher usually specify that the author will retain the contract. Contracts from university, academic, and other small presses, however, often grant the publisher the right to register the copyright in the publisher's name. Since this clause may be negotiable, authors should ask. Casebook publishers seek to retain the copyright so that they can continue to publish editions even if an author dies, retires or simply decides that he or she no longer wants to update his or her book.

The "Rights and Royalties" clauses are critical for authors. If a publisher has only the capacity to publish a book in English and distribute it in Canada and the United States, authors should be reluctant to grant the publisher the right to publish the book in any translation throughout the world. The author may be able to exploit this right with a separate publisher for more income. Authors can separate the rights by languages and by countries and, for example, sell Spanish language rights in Spain and Latin American countries.

Additionally, publishers may see audio, audiovisual, electronic, film, television, and digital media rights. Some contracts may specify all rights currently in existence and any other rights that may come into existence to take into account changing technology. Contracts that used to specify "world rights" are now being changed to refer to the "universe" because of satellite transmission.

Major conglomerates with movie, television, music, game and other entertainment divisions have swallowed up many independent publishers. Highly connected publishers may seek film and television rights that they can shop to one of their divisions. Authors who consent may obtain a quicker sale, but perhaps with less revenue than if their agents sell these rights separately. Several New York literary agents, for example, maintain connections with Hollywood agents to service their author clients in this manner.

Rights are also intimately tied to compensation.

3. ROYALTY PROVISIONS

Trade publishers typically offer a royalty fee of 10 to 20 percent on the retail price for hardcover books, but less for paperback, and even less for mass-market paperback books. To fall into the latter category, publishers print 500,000 copies or more of a book, while offering authors a 5 percent royalty. They sell these deeply discounted books in markets like Costco, K-Mart, Wal-Mart, and Sam's Club. Some writers or their agents can negotiate a royalty schedule. After the first 10,000, 50,000, 100,000 or more in sales, the royalty fee increases according to an agreed-upon scale.

Smaller presses tend to be independent, university, and academic operations. They offer payment on net proceeds because they sell fewer copies and therefore receive less revenue. The royalty rate may range from 10 – 20% of net proceeds. The challenge for authors, their agents and attorneys, is to understand the publisher's definition of net proceeds.

Fortunately, the definition of net proceeds in the publishing industry is more likely to produce revenue than in the movie industry, where "net profits" may be termed a figment of some accountant's imagination. For example, one academic publisher defines net proceeds as:

> "the actual price received by the Publisher from all sales whether retail or trade (wholesale) sales.   The total of these sales shall be reduced by the amount of credits, actual returns, and a reasonable reserve for anticipated returns of 20%."

From this clause, the authors will receive higher royalties if the publisher sells the work at its retail price directly off its website or through mail order. The royalties will be noticeably less when the publisher wholesales the book to a bookstore or another website. The more aggressive the definitions of net profit, the more often authors try to negotiate a higher royalty payment of at least 15-20%

When publishers purchase other rights, they may ask to split the film or television rights 50-50. Since the publisher is, in effect, acting as the author's agent, authors have been known to negotiate a more profitable (60-40, 75-25, or 85-15) split with the publisher.

4. ACCOUNTING PROVISIONS

Accounting provisions indicate when authors can expect to receive royalty checks. The accountings may be monthly, quarterly, semi-annually or annually. The smaller the press, the lengthier will be accounting periods. The publisher will offer to send the payments within 30 to 90 days following the close of the accounting period.

These provisions may be difficult to negotiate because they often depend on the publisher's overall accounting practices. However, trade publishers have been known to provide shorter accounting periods for their best-selling authors who are generating a great deal of revenue. If the author does not yet fall into this category, the agent or attorney can ask for a shorter period, but the publisher is likely to resist setting up a different system for a lesser-known author.

5. WARRANTIES

As discussed earlier, magazine and book publishers may require authors to warrant certain conditions about their manuscripts. Warranty clauses may require the author to guarantee to the publisher that:

* The author is the sole creator and owner of the work
* The work has not been previously published
* The work does not violate another work's copyright
* The work does not violate anyone's right of privacy
* The work does not libel or defame anyone
* The work does not violate any government regulation

If the author's work violates any of the above warranties, the publisher reserves the right to cancel the contract.

Warranty clauses are often accompanied by an indemnity provision, asking the author to indemnify, or repay, the publisher should the work violate a warranty provision. If the publisher is sued because of the author's work, the author must defend the lawsuit and reimburse the publisher for any of its related expenses.

6. EXPENSES, PERMISSIONS & FAIR USE

Publishers may grant authors a budget to cover certain expenses, such as those connected with travel, interviews, or obtaining permission to use other people's work. The type and amount of such expenses may be negotiated depending on the type of project.

Authors who quote substantially from other authors' copyrighted works should obtain permission from the copyright holder, who is usually the author or the publisher. Some copyright holders will grant the right to republish part or all of an article or book without payment. Others may request substantial fees for this right, although authors can always attempt to negotiate a lower rate than that which was initially quoted.

For some quotations and reprints authors may claim a fair-use privilege to use another's work. Uses of another's work that are considered fair include quoting the work to critique or comment it. In such a case permission is not required, as authors would rarely grant permission to use their work in a harsh manner. Determining whether or not the fair-use privilege applies requires authors to use their best judgment, while understanding the dictates of 17 U.S.C. 107, as discussed in Chapter 2. Authors using a work for educational purposes have more leeway than those who just plan to profit from another person's labor. Nevertheless, authors must keep in mind that if the copyright owner sues, the author may have to pay to defend both himself and his publisher.

7. EDITIONS, AUTHOR COPIES, OUT OF PRINT

A publishing contract may also specify that the publisher receive the first right to publish further editions of the work. Authors of a continuing series (such as mysteries) and textbook publications should be aware that such clauses gives the publisher the right to name other writers to produce additional editions. This may be so even with newspaper columns. When Ann Landers died, her column expired with her. Yet when Dear Abby, Ann's twin sister, became too feeble to write, the column was passed on to her daughter.

The author's copies clause specifies how many free copies of the book will be sent to the author, and the cost of any additional copies the author may want to purchase. Sometimes these clauses specify that the author cannot resell reduced-price copies. Other times, they are silent on this issue, which means that authors can resell such copies. Authors may attempt to elaborate on the circumstances where re-sales would be permitted, such as when selling copies at a lecture, conference, or book signing.

Publishing contracts often provide that when the book goes out of print, and the publisher refuses to print more upon written request, all rights will revert to the author. Some contracts permit the authors to buy back any remaining copies and the plates that were used to produce the manuscript.

8. ASSIGNMENT

A clause that has become standard in the era of mergers and acquisitions is the assignment clause, granting the publisher the right to assign the contract to another publisher. Authors may sell their book to Publisher A only to have Publisher Q purchase or merge with Publisher A soon thereafter. With an assignment clause, Publisher Q assumes the responsibility for publishing the book. The author remains protected because the book will still be available, although the publisher changes.

9. PRINT ON DEMAND & INTERNET SALES

In search of quick production at low cost, authors are turning to print on demand publishers. For reasonable set-up fees, iUniverse, Xlibris, Authorhouse, and many other Internet publishers will format authors' books and sell copies for them on an order-first/then-print basis. Authors who choose the POD route can purchase their own books at a 40% discount and they receive royalties when other people buy their books.

The POD publishing route is unlikely to produce significant revenue for writers. The Writer magazine reports that Xlibris has sold an average of 33 books of its 9,000 printed titles, and out of iUniverse's 17,000 titles, only 84 have sold more than 500 copies. Further, only about six of iUniverse's titles have made it on to the bookshelves of Barnes & Noble, which owns 25% of iUniverse. *See* Moira Allen, *Measuring the value of POD: Make sure print on demand is right for you*, THE WRITER, June 2004, at 15-16.

When POD publishers sell books through an Internet reseller, like Amazon.com, authors receive a reduced royalty. Amazon.com has become a billion-dollar corporation by reselling new and used books, and other entertainment products, at discounts through its website. Jonathon Miller, the author of *Rattlesnake Lawyer*, says writers should "be aware that they will receive no royalties for used books resold through Amazon.com." He adds, "Writers also need to know that their ranking on Amazon.com is crucial. I know some unscrupulous publishers and authors who try to manipulate their ranking by urging their friends to buy books through Amazon.com."

The advantage to achieving the number 1 ranking on Amazon.com is that other publications use the Amazon.com numbers to compute their best-seller lists. Certain bookstores, like those found in airports, are much more likely to order books appearing on the New York Times or other major publications' best-seller lists.

In conclusion, all contracts for entertainers offer their benefits and burdens. It's up to entertainers and their lawyers to discover what these are and proceed accordingly.

CHAPTER 9

CELEBRITY STATUS

Obtaining national and global eminence brings advantages and disadvantages to entertainers. This celebrity status blesses them with access to more resources. They can capitalize on their names and images by exploiting their right of publicity. Some celebrities use their prominence to run for political office or advance a social agenda. Other entertainers capitalize on the sudden availability of ordinary mortals seeking sexual relations with them. Sometimes they pay a price for their excesses in paternity suits or criminal actions brought against them. Some celebrities who are dissatisfied with their level of wealth have succumbed to greed, which has ultimately landed them in jail.

Taking on celebrity clients test lawyers' abilities in a myriad of ways. A long-celebrated personality is more likely to view the lawyer as hired help and less likely to follow advice. This places attorneys in uncomfortable situations, particularly when clients seem determined to pursue unlawful activities. Some lawyers bite the bullet and fire clients. Others go along and may find themselves sent to prison along with their clients, although probably in a less comfortable facility.

This chapter addresses a number of issues associated with celebrity status. It first sets up the advantages and disadvantages that accompany celebrity status. This gives the attorney a broader sense of the peculiarities associated with the accomplished entertainer's life.

Second, this chapter highlights celebrities' rights to privacy and publicity. The glitter of bright lights fades as entertainers find their privacy constantly violated by overzealous fans and a hyperactive media. Associated with the right to privacy is the right to publicity, which permits celebrities to capitalize on their names and images by endorsing products. The right to privacy expires with the death of the celebrity. The right to publicity survives the celebrity's demise and descends to his or her heirs at law by intestate succession or by any person or entity the celebrity chooses to designate by will or trust.

Because of the value attached to the rights of publicity and other forms of intellectual property, this chapter concludes by briefly discussing estate-planning issues for celebrities. More and more entertainers plan their estates to take advantage of their income earning potential after their deaths. A number of celebrities earn more money after their demise than they did while living. This increases the need for attorneys to explore estate-planning issues with their celebrity clients.

A. ADVANTAGES & DISADVANTAGES

Becoming a celebrity in this era of history generates economic rewards and fame where, to quote the *Cheers* theme song, "everyone knows your name." Several entertainers have used their fame to fulfill political ambitions, rising to become mayors of cities, governors in the states of California and Minnesota, congressmen, senators, and even president of the United States. The 1987 film *Running Man*, based on a Stephen King novel, was the first movie to feature two future governors, Arnold Schwarzenegger and Jesse Ventura, in a fight scene. The honorable governor of California won. Virginian John Warner married actress Elizabeth Taylor just prior to launching his senate campaign. The crowds came out in droves, he won, and the couple later divorced.

When Robert Redford first started discussing the environment in the 1960s, he was dismissed out of hand. "He's only an actor," was an often-uttered comment. "Then came Ronald Reagan, and Arnold," said Redford. "People began to take note." Now people show up in droves to hear Redford bemoan the destruction of the environment. He told several hundred souls who assembled at the Randall Davey Audubon Center in Santa Fe, New Mexico, on July 14, 2004, "I'm here today to try to raise awareness, to try to stop this avalanche." He called for "responsible development, to get us into a sustainable future." His comments were greeted with sustained applause.

Some individuals who achieve wealth through the entertainment industry give away their money. According to lawyer turned television mogul Jim Rogers, "Once you've passed the buying and accumulating stage and you're not interested in pursuing contests of adding more commas and zeroes to your financial statement, all that's left is to give it away." Rogers says there "is no greater feeling than the joy that flows from giving."

Rogers donated $115 million to the University of Arizona in 1998, making national headlines as the largest gift ever to a law school. To express its gratitude, the institution renamed itself the James E. Rogers College of Law. Dean Toni Massaro said that Rogers' gift brought "hope, excitement, and a renewed commitment to acting on our better ideas."

With that gift, Rogers' status elevated from generous donor to philanthropist. In its July 24, 2000, edition, Time Magazine ran "The New Philanthropists" as its cover story and proclaimed Rogers as number 12 among the country's top philanthropists. This list includes Bill and Melinda Gates who have donated $22 billion to their foundation, and Ted Turner, founder of CNN, who gave a billion dollars to the United Nations Foundation.

From his office in Las Vegas in the fall of 2000, Rogers explained his simple philosophy of giving. "You start with the premise that most great fortunes are earned by a group of people influenced by a convergence of circumstances, so that no one person can take 100% credit for creating it. Then you find that after you've accumulated so much, there are only so many cars, houses, boats, and planes that you can buy, and after you've bought them, you find you don't use them."

Rogers is also known to touch individual lives with anonymous small gifts. Sometimes his television station KVBC employees have dined at Las Vegas restaurants unaware that Rogers was present until they call for their check only to be informed that a Mr. James E. Rogers had already paid their tab.

Unfortunately, national prominence can bring disadvantages. Jon Moritsugu directed the 1999 film *Fame Whore* to challenge, he said, "a naïve view that once you're famous... everything will fall into place. Fame can be a particularly deadly drug." *Arts Talk* (Olelo Television broadcast, 1999).

During their lives and immediately following their deaths, some celebrities have individuals come forth claiming to be related. After Marlon Brando achieved national prominence in the movie version of *Street Car Named Desire*, he told NBC executive Brandon Tartikoff what happened to him:

"For a year ... I never touched a door. I couldn't touch a door if I wanted to. People were opening them for me. I could show up at the fanciest restaurant at the busiest hour and they'd say, 'Right this way.' I'd sit up in my house in the Hollywood Hills getting bombed, and I'd be watching the news at ten p.m. and I'd see this blond woman doing the news and I'd call up the station. I'd ask to get her on the phone, and I'd say, 'Hi, sweetheart, this is Marlon Brando. I think you're real attractive. How'd you like to come over to my place when you're done?' And sure enough, she'd be over at my house about a half hour later, and I'd be in bed with her. It was just like ordering Chinese food. That was Hollywood, and it was great.

Tartikoff, *supra* note 6, at 23. Brando's ability to order up women was not without consequence. After he died at the age of 80 on July 1, 2004, a London paper reported that he might have had eight illegitimate children in addition to the 11 he acknowledged in his will. *See* Dan Evans, *Brando's Eight Secret Children*, SUNDAY MIRROR, July 4, 2004. One sobbing 40-year-old actress demanded to be let into the actor's home so she could take her place among her siblings, but was turned away by security guards. *Id.*

Tennis star Boris Becker was hit with a paternity suit while still married to his pregnant wife Barbara. At a posh London restaurant,

Becker dallied in a broom closet with Russian model Angela Ermakova. The result was a baby linked to Becker through a DNA test. At trial, he claimed that the model was hired to hold him down and steal his sperm.[32] The judge awarded the model $1.5 million to care for the child. Becker also paid his wife Barbara $14.4 million to settle their divorce.

Sports stars seem particularly vulnerable to the hordes of women who lie in wait after their games or in the lobby of their hotels seeking sexual relations with them. At least one woman claimed her sexual interactions with Los Angeles Laker Kobe Bryant were not consensual. He was charged with rape. More often, however, women with dollar signs dancing behind their eyes play the pregnancy game. They entice sports stars into sexual encounters in hopes of having a baby. As in the Boris Becker incident, the payoff can be huge. Women have filed paternity suits against basketball stars Larry Bird, Patrick Ewing, Jason Kidd, and Scottie Pippen. Shawn Kemp allegedly fathered seven illegitimate children, only to have their mothers hit him with millions of dollars in claims for support.

Sports stars and organizations have noticed this trend and taken action. Some basketball stars are known to mentor their younger

---

[32] For more information, *see* Sherri Burr, *Courts hear new angle on the law of sex: sperm theft*, ALBUQUERQUE TRIBUNE, Aug. 30, 2001, at C.1.

brethren to urge them to avoid ensnarement with women seeking to have their children. The National Football League currently provides its rookies with a life talk during training camp to counsel them on this issue.

While paternity suits present challenges to lawyers, keeping some clients out of jail can be time consuming. Television host Martha Stewart convinced herself that she knew what she was doing when she spoke to federal prosecutors investigating her for securities fraud. Stewart thought she had nothing to hide. Along with her co-defendant Peter E. Bacanovic, she was convicted of conspiracy, obstruction, and lying to investigators. U.S. District Court judge Miriam Goldman Cedarbaum sentenced both Stewart and Bacanovic to five months in prison and five months of home confinement. The judge recommended that Stewart serve time in a minimum-security federal work camp in Danbury, Connecticut, which is situated 20 miles from Stewart's Connecticut home, and permitted her to remain free pending appeal.

An argument can be made that Stewart was done in by greed, with karmic consequences. She saved $45,000 in the stock trade that brought the eyes of the prosecutors upon her. After she was indicted, her billion-dollar company lost half its value. Upon her conviction, Viacom cancelled her television show *Martha Stewart Living*, which had been on the air on stations covering 85% of the country since 1991.

Ironically, after she was sentenced, bargain hunters bid up shares of Martha Stewart Living Omnimedia by 37% during heavy trading. After Stewart received a short sentence, some traders bet the company may rebound. They are taking a chance. The company's direction will be in limbo for several years if she appeals her conviction. Further, if Stewart succeeds in obtaining a new trial and gets convicted again, her next sentence could be lengthier, which would threaten the company's stock price.

When television stars like Robert Blake and O.J. Simpson are charged with murder, their attorneys must not only investigate their criminal cases but they must augment their media skills to address the increased interest in their client's fate. Attorneys possessing such skills are in high demand. Thomas Mesereau Jr. represented Blake before they parted ways in a dispute. Mersereau was then hired by Michael Jackson to represent him on child molestation charges after Jackson released Mark Geragos. Geragos had represented movie star Winona Ryder on shoplifting charges. She was convicted.

Attorneys sometimes need to gag their clients for their own good. Instead of appearing at his arraignment quietly, Michael Jackson danced on top of a car and his family stoked the fans' interest by inviting them to his home for a picnic. Being charged with a crime brought an about face for Jackson who had jealously guarded his privacy and that of his children. He and his kids previously wore masks to prevent the media from obtaining full-faced photographs.

B. PRIVACY & PUBLICITY RIGHTS

Stardom and superstardom can bring a sudden and dramatic loss of privacy. Some overnight celebrities resort to shopping for the necessities of life at midnight where they are unlikely to be disturbed at their neighborhood grocery store. Reality television star Bob Guiney acknowledges that he cannot complain about the loss of privacy that accompanied his appearances on the ABC series *The Bachelorette* and *The Bachelor*. He says, "I did this to myself." *See* Burr and Henslee, *supra* note 1, at 324.

While all individuals have a right to privacy, celebrities trade a measure of their rights for fame and thus what others can say about them is broader than for ordinary mortals. For example, there is no First Amendment protection of the media to publish defamatory statements about public officials and public figures with actual malice, "either with knowledge of their falsity or reckless disregard for the truth." *See* Eastwood v. The Superior Court of Los Angeles County, 149 Cal.App.3d 409, 424 (Cal. Ct. App. 1983). A private individual, however, can sue for defamatory statements published with negligence. *Id.*

State law protects the right of privacy. Dean Prosser describes it as four distinct torts: (1)

intrusion upon the plaintiff's seclusion or solitude, or into his private affairs; (2) public disclosure of embarrassing private facts about the plaintiff; (3) publicity which places the plaintiff in a false light in the public eye; and (4) appropriation, for the defendant's advantage, of plaintiff's name and likeness. Prosser, *Privacy*, 48 CAL. L. REV. 383, 384 (1960), *quoted in* Eastwood, 149 Cal. App.3d at 416.

After the National Enquirer published an article headlined "Clint Eastwood in Love Triangle," Eastwood sued the paper, claiming that it violated his right to privacy, particularly under Prosser's fourth category. California Civil Code Sec. 3344 supplements that provision by providing:

"Any person who knowingly uses another's name, photograph, or likeness, in any manner, for purposes of advertising products, merchandise, goods, or services, or for purposes of solicitation of purchases of products ... without such person's prior consent ... shall be liable for any damages sustained by the person ... injured as a result thereof."

Eastwood, 149 Cal. App.3d at 417. Eastwood charged that the National Enquirer had placed him in a false light in the public eye by publishing an untrue article stating that he was caught in a love triangle between singer Tanya Tucker and actress Sandra Locke. The court agreed, concluding that the Enquirer violated his common law and section 3344(a) rights when it "commercially exploited his name, photograph, and likeness." *Id.* at 421.

Because Eastwood alleged that the Enquirer appropriated his name and likeness to sell their story, he also invoked the right of publicity. The right of publicity is a property interest grounded in three separate legal sources: state statutes, common law, and the federal unfair competition act. When someone else profits from an entertainer's name, image, or voice, this affects the celebrity in a number of ways, but most importantly the entertainer loses some control over his image, particularly when the use presents false material.

In considering Eastwood's case, the court examined the juxtaposition between the right of privacy and the public's right to know. Because freedom of the press is constitutionally guaranteed, the court observed, "a celebrity relinquishes a part of his right to privacy to the extent that the public has a legitimate interest in his doings, affairs, or character. The accomplishments and way of life of such persons may legitimately be mentioned and discussed in print." *Id.* at 412. Nevertheless, the court noted that First Amendment rights "do not require total abrogation of the right of privacy or the right of publicity." *Id.* at 422.

The distinction between the media's responsibility to investigate statements about public figures and ordinary citizens turned out to be an important one for Eastwood. He did not initially allege that the article was published with knowledge of falsity or with reckless disregard for the truth as required for media statements on public figures. The court granted him leave to amend his complaint to cure this defect. *Id.* at 426.

Unlike the right of publicity, the right of privacy expires upon death and cannot be evoked on behalf of the deceased by his survivors. In *Maritote v. Desilu Productions, Inc.*, 345 F.2d 418 (7th Cir. 1965), the court said, "It is anomalous to speak of the privacy of a deceased person." In *Maritote*, the widow and son of mobster Al Capone claimed that Desilu Productions violated his privacy right by exploiting his image for commercial advantages when it produced a two-part drama and television series called *The Untouchables*. The court quoted Shakespeare, "the evil that men do lives after them." *Id.* at 420. It further added, "What a man does while alive becomes a part of history which survives his death." *Id.*

Not only do the deceased not possess privacy rights, neither can his relatives sue for violation of their privacy rights if they are not mentioned in a comment, fictionalization, or even distortion of a dead man's career. *Id.* The court refused to enjoin Desilu's use of Al Capone's name and image.

The right of publicity, nevertheless, can be exploited during the celebrity's lifetime and after his or her death. Several television stars, including Johnny Carson and Vanna White, have successfully enjoined the commercial exploitation of their image. Johnny Carson was able to stop a company from marketing "Here's Johnny" portable toilets because that phrase was Johnny Carson's signature introduction on *The Tonight Show. See* Carson v. Here's Johnny Portable Toilets, Inc., 698 F.2d 831 (6th Cir. 1983).

In *White v. Samsung Electronics America,* 971 F.2d 1395 (9th Cir. 1992), the Ninth Circuit held that the right of publicity extends to the name, likeness, voice, signature, and anything else that evokes the person's identity. For *Wheel of Fortune* star Vanna White, the latter category included a Samsung advertisement featuring "a robot, dressed in a wig, gown, and jewelry … consciously selected to resemble White's hair and dress. The robot was posed next to a game board which is instantly recognizable as the *Wheel of Fortune* game show set, in a stance for which White is famous." *Id.* at 1396. The Ninth Circuit held that White was entitled to pursue Samsung because the law protects the celebrity's sole right to exploit the value associated with his or her name that has been created with energy and ingenuity. *Id.* at 1399.

Cheers actors George Wendt and John Ratzenberger sued Host International to keep them from creating animatronic robot figures based on their likeness and placing them in airport bars modeled to resemble the *Cheer's* set without their permission. *See* Wendt v. Host International, 125 F.3d 806 (9th Cir. 1997). Having the robots emulate the Norm and Cliff characters meant they resembled Wendt and Ratzenberger who embodied those characters on *Cheers.* The Ninth Circuit ruled that the actors were at least entitled to a jury trial to determine whether Host International was commercially exploiting their likeness.

Sports stars find their achievements magnified by television. Consequently, many can make more money from their endorsement contracts than from playing their respective sports. Protecting their trademark names and right to publicity is important to both unsuccessful and successful athletes. Anna Kournikova, who never won a tennis tournament during her short-lived career, earned millions of dollars from advertising endorsements that take advantage of her attractive looks.

Basketball legend Kareem Abdul-Jabbar sued General Motors Corporation for using his birth name Lew Alcindor to advertise an Oldsmobile. *See* Abdul-Jabbar v. General Motors Corporation, 85 F.3d 407 (9th Cir. 1996). Abdul-Jabbar argued GMC's use of his birth name falsely implied that he had endorsed its products. GMC countered that Abdul-Jabbar had abandoned the name Lew Alcindor when he formerly recorded the Abdul-Jabbar name under an Illinois statute.

In reversing the district court's grant of summary judgment for GMC, the court of appeals observed that because a birth name is an integral part of identity, it is not bestowed for commercial purposes and thus cannot be deemed "abandoned" when its possessor discontinues using it. *Id.* at 408. The court said, "California's common law right of publicity protects celebrities from appropriation of their *identity* not strictly definable as 'name or picture'." *Id.* at 415.

As noted earlier in the discussion of the *Eastwood* case, the court balances the right of publicity with the First Amendment right of freedom of expression. Professional golfer Tiger Woods sued the Jireh Publishing Company and artist Rich Rush for reproducing artwork that included his image and used his name to identify the work. In *ETW Corporation v. Jireh Publishing, Inc.*, 332 F.3d 915 (6th Cir. 2003), Woods claimed that that the company violated his trademark "Tiger Woods" and his right of publicity. The court of appeals disagreed. It noted that "[a] celebrity's name may be used in the title of an artistic work so long as there is some artistic relevance." *Id.* at 920. In this instance, the court said that the "use of Woods' name on the back of the envelope containing the print and in the narrative description of that print are purely descriptive and there is nothing to indicate that they were used other than in good faith." *Id.*

The court was also careful to distinguish Woods' name as a valid trademark from his image, which is not protected as a trademark when it does not distinguish and identify the source of goods. As a general rule, the court said, "a person's image or likeness cannot function as a trademark." *Id.* at 921.

Further, a person cannot protect his image as a publicity right if to do so would run afoul of another person's First Amendment rights. For example, a person's name and likeness can be used in news reporting. *Id.* at 930. The court noted that Woods' 1997 Masters victory was an historic event in the world of sports, and art "communicates and celebrates the value our culture attaches to such events." *Id.* at 936. The court found that Rush's artwork was "entitled to the full protection of the First Amendment.... Through their pervasive presence in the media, sports and entertainment celebrities have come to symbolize certain ideas and values in our society and have become a valuable means of expression in our culture." *Id.* at 937.

One final note on privacy and publicity rights is related to the growing crime of identity theft. Frank Abagnale, author of *The Art of the Steal*, terms identity theft "the mother of all scams, because it steals everything, a person's very being."[33] The Internet makes celebrities vulnerable because con artists can discover information about them through publicly

---

[33] FRANK ABAGNALE, THE ART OF THE STEAL 203 (2001).

available sources. Thieves seek to capitalize on the wealth associated with a famous name by stealing the person's credit cards and personal information. They then impersonate the person, using their identifying factors such as social security and drivers license numbers to buy clothes, furniture, cars, and real estate. Abagnale published the book *Identity Theft* in August 2004 to bring even more attention to the hazards of the crime.

On July 15, 2004, President Bush signed the Identity Theft Penalty Enhancement Act, which adds two years to prison sentences for criminals convicted of using stolen credit card numbers and other personal data to commit crimes. "Like other forms of stealing, identity theft leaves the victim poorer and feeling terribly violated," Bush said. "The criminal can quickly damage a person's lifelong effort to build a good credit rating." David McGuire, *Bush Signs Identity Theft Bill*, WASH. POST, July 15, 2004.

C. ESTATE PLANNING

In October 2003, www.forbes.com published its annual list of top-earning deceased celebrities with their names, their principal occupation during their lifetime, and how many millions of dollars their estate made during the preceding year:

Elvis Presley	(singer)	$40
Charles Schulz	(cartoonist, *Peanuts*)	$32
J.R.R. Tolkien	(author, *The Hobbit*)	$22

John Lennon	(singer, The Beatles)	$19
George Harrison	(singer, The Beatles)	$16
Theodor Geisel	(author, *Doctor Seuss*)	$16
Dale Earnhardt	(race car driver)	$15
Tupac Shakur	(singer, rap)	$12
Bob Marley	(singer, reggae)	$9
Marilyn Monroe	(movie actress)	$8

Incredibly, many of their estates earn more than the celebrities did during their lifetimes. During her 36 years of life, Marilyn Monroe earned less than $1 million in total, yet her estate now generates as much as eight times that amount in one year. Part of the increase is due to inflation, but a significant portion is due to her attainment of legend status.

Since Tupac Shakur perished from a gunshot wound in September 1996, he has starred in five movies, including the 2003 feature documentary *Resurrection* produced with footage filmed before his death. Shakur has also released more albums after his death than before, leading to street rumors that he must still be alive. Similarly the many "sightings" of Elvis around the world since his 1977 death from an overdose of drugs have only increased his allure and the revenue earnings of his estate.

Because of the substantial earning potential of their estates after their death, some renowned figures carefully plan ahead. Dr. Martin Luther King, Jr. was known to copyright all his speeches. In 1963, he sued Mister Maestro, Inc.

to restrain them from selling phonograph records of his "I have a Dream" speech. Dr. King delivered the speech on August 28, 1963, which he had just finished writing that morning. He mailed in the copyright registration form on September 30, 1963. *See* King v. Mister Maestro, Inc. 224 F.Supp. 101 (S.D.N.Y. 1963). After his assassination in 1968, King's estate was valued at $66,492.29. It is now worth several million dollars and supports his surviving wife and children. *See* Sherri Burr, *Don't leave Earth without it: why writers need a will*, EDITOR & WRITER 56 (Nov./Dec. 1997).

To die intestate, without a will, or testate, with a will, is the celebrity's choice. The next sections examine the differences in outcome between the two choices for the celebrity's heirs.

1. INTESTATE SUCCESSION

In any given year, approximately two-thirds of all Americans die without a will. In the year 2000, the number of adults who had a will approached an all time high of 47%, but this number declined to 42% by 2004, according to legal publishers Martindale-Hubble.[34] The company cited procrastination as a common culprit for people not drafting a will, along with concerns about declining assets and estate tax uncertainties.[35]

---

[34] Kathy Chu, *Fewer Estates Exercise Will Power*, WALL S. J., June 10, 2004, at D.1.
[35] *Id.*

Whatever the reason, the number of Americans dying intestate includes such luminaries as film financier Howard Hughes, movie star James Dean, and President Abraham Lincoln, who authored many memorable documents but not his own will. By dying intestate, individuals risk having their estate decided by the state or through a lawsuit.

After Howard Hughes' death in 1976, thousands of individuals claiming to be distant relatives and illegitimate children sought a share of his $6 billion estate. One fake will caused Hollywood to memorialize the tale surrounding its creation into the film *Melvin and Howard*. The brawl over Hughes estate was finally settled in 1996 with layers taking a hefty share, more than $20 million in fees. *See* Sherri L. Burr, *Don't leave Earth without it: why writers need a will*, EDITOR & WRITER 56 (Nov./Dec. 1997). For an interesting story about the estate's bizarre twists and turns, see James R. Phelan and Lewis Chester's *The Money: The Battle for Howard Hughes's Billions* (1997).

States allocate the deceased entertainer's remaining assets to their nearest relatives, unless there are none and then the assets will escheat or be consumed by the state. All states have adopted plans to distribute an estate in the event a person dies without a will. Eighteen states have adopted the Uniform Probate Code (UPC), which divides the estate among the nearest surviving relatives. The UPC gives the surviving spouse the deceased person's entire estate if no parents or descendants (children, grandchildren, etc.) survive the dead person, or if the surviving spouse and the deceased shared all the surviving children. The UPC also takes into consideration the decedent and the surviving spouse's prior and subsequent marriages that produced offspring.

If there are parents or descendants, then the surviving spouse may only receive the most significant part of the estate and the others may receive a share. In addition to parents and descendants, the UPC will give assets to siblings, grandparents, aunts, uncles, and cousins. Some states have laws that will look at the person's family tree as far as the great-grand parent level. To change the state's intestate default plan, the person must write a will to leave resources to foundations, friends, or more distant relatives.

2. WILLS

To write a valid will, the celebrity must meet three criteria. He or she must (1) be at least 18 years of age; (2) be of sound mind; and (3) sign and date the will according to the state's requirements. Several states permit a person to prepare holographic wills, which means the material provisions are entirely in the person's handwriting. If the will is typed, then there must be at least two witnesses (some states require three) who observe the decedent sign and date the will, and they sign and date the will in the decedent's presence and in the presence of each other. In some states, the witnesses must be disinterested, that is they will receive nothing from the will. Under the UPC, they may be interested or disinterested.

The requirements are simple and the advantages are important to the celebrity's family or other persons or entities the celebrity wishes to leave part of his or her estate. For example, section 201(d) of the U.S. Copyright Act specifically provides that the ownership of copyright may be "bequeathed by will or pass as personal property by the applicable laws of intestate succession." The celebrity can give all of his copyrights to a particular family member or to a charity. The celebrity possesses the choice.

Estate planning preserves the rights of celebrities to continue to capitalize on their image and valuable intellectual property after their deaths. In 1616, Shakespeare crafted a will giving away his estate primarily to his wife, son, and daughter. Shakespeare penned his sonnets and plays before England passed the Statute of Anne, the world's first Copyright Law in 1710.

Prior to committing suicide in 1962, Marilyn Monroe signed a two-page will leaving her estate to her mother, half-sister, and friends. While none of the specific gifts mentioned exceeded $100,000, the gift of her personal effects and clothing to her acting coach Lee Strasberg, who later left them to his wife Anna, turned out to be a goldmine. Valued at $3,200 at the time of Monroe's death, the items were auctioned off by Christie's New York in 1999 for $13.4 million after the death of Anna Strasberg.[36]

During their lifetimes, both Strasbergs were careful to maintain Monroe's privacy by not disposing of her property or permitting media access to Monroe's letters or documents. In 1996, Anna Strasberg sued the heir of Monroe's former manager to keep him from auctioning off some of Monroe's personal effects. *See* Strasberg v. Odyssey Group, Inc., 51 Cal. App. 4th 906, 59 Cal. Rptr. 2d 474 (Cal. Ct. App. 1996). Strasberg claimed she was the present sole beneficiary of Monroe's personal effects under Monroe's will and sought a constructive trust over the items. The court agreed and ordered the items returned to Strasberg.

Currently, Monroe's estate receives its revenues primarily from licensing and royalty deals. Monroe's image is used on posters, T-shirts, checkbook covers, Venetian blinds, cookie jars, Christmas ornaments, shoulder pads, camera straps and stockings.[37] According to the estate's official website, Monroe's face has graced promotional campaigns all over the world, including for Mercedes Benz in the

---

[36] Damion Matthews, *Freudians Prefer Blondes*, SALON PEOPLE, Nov. 10, 1999, *available at* http://www.salon.com/people/feature/1000/1 1/10/marilyn/

[37] *Id.*

United Sates, Levi's jeans in Germany, and Nestlé in the United Kingdom.[38]

Singers John Lennon and Elvis Presley left the bulk of their estates to their families. Lennon took into consideration tax issues in leaving his estate to his widow Yoko Ono. The second clause of the will establishes one-half of estate to qualify for the marital deduction. He named his wife and his friend Eli Garber as trustees of the remainder of the estate and appointed her as guardian of their children. Lennon did not make any references to his first-born son Julian Lennon, the product of his first marriage to Cynthia Lennon.

By writing a will, celebrities may add clauses that disinherit someone, either by name or by category. In his will, Elvis Presley left the remainder of his estate in a residuary trust for his "lawful children." He also directed his trustee to pay maintenance and support for his daughter "Lisa Marie Presley, and any other lawful issue I might have." When Deborah Delaine Presley came forward in 1989 claiming to be Presley' illegitimate child, the court held that his will expressly excluded her because she was not born during Presley's marriage to her mother. Indeed, he never married her mother. *See* Presley v. Hanks, 782 S.W.2d 482 (Ten. Ct. App. 1989).

---

[38] http://www.marilynmonroe.com/about/view-headline.php?id-2549.

The issue of whether Deborah Delaine was actually Presley's daughter became irrelevant. In Tennessee, the court noted that words such as "children" in a will are construed to mean legitimate children and do not include illegitimate children. *Id.* at 490. To include illegitimate children in Tennessee, Presley would need to have expressly done so. Instead, he did the opposite. Thus, either way Delaine was left without a valid legal claim to a share of Presley's estate.

3. TRUSTS

Elvis Presley signed his will a few months before his death in 1977, leaving the bulk of his estate in support trusts for his daughter Lisa Marie Presley, grandmother Minnie Mae Presley, father Vernon E. Presley, and other relatives living at the time who may need emergency assistance while his father is alive. After the death of his father, these beneficiaries were eliminated from support. The trust for Lisa Marie terminated on her 25th birthday and she received all the assets outright.

The trusts that Presley created in his will are considered testamentary trusts. Trusts may also be set up during the person's lifetime. They are called intervivos trusts. Such trusts permit flexible management of assets during the person's lifetime. Because they often include payable on death provisions, they avoid the probate process. Because wills are public documents, several celebrities create trusts so that the public will not know, unless there is a lawsuit, how they chose to dispose of their assets.

There is, however, a mistaken assumption that intervivos trusts also avoid taxes. They do not. The IRS will calculate the celebrity's gross estate in deciding whether or not the estate tax is due. For years 2004-2005, there is no effective tax due on the first $1,500,000 of assets. For years 2006-2008, the first 2,000,000 of assets are effectively excluded from tax. In year 2009, the first $3,500,000 is effectively excluded from estate tax. In year 2010, the estate tax is eliminated. By year 2011, the estate tax will revert to the year 2000 rates, which effectively excluded tax on the first $675,000 worth of assets.

The estate tax affects very few estates. In 1997, when the first $600,000 worth of assets was effectively excluded from taxation, less than 43,000 estates owed taxes. This number represented less than 1.9 percent of the 2.3 million people who died that year. Since accomplished celebrities may die with considerable assets, they can benefit the most from planning their estates in advance.

CHAPTER 10

GLOBALIZATION

The United States entertainment industry is a global enterprise. The M.P.A.A., a trade association comprised of the leading film studios, estimates that U.S. films are shown in more than 150 countries worldwide and television shows can be found in over 125 international markets. All forms of music emanating from the United States are routinely sold abroad. The London theater district often sends its plays to Broadway and vice versa. Russian and African dance troops are as likely to tour the United States as the Alvin Ailey troop is to perform in Paris. United States' citizens enhance the culture of others and are themselves enriched by the culture of others.

This chapter sets up the problem of global piracy and then addresses the ongoing internationalization of the entertainment business and the legal consequences that flow there from. Nations in the early stages of economic development have an incentive to encourage the pilfering of intellectual property creations like films, television shows and music, as their citizens are enlightened without having to pay the full price.

A. GLOBAL PIRACY

Prior to World War II, the United States was a net importer of intellectual property and its citizens actively pirated works produced in other countries. Charles Dickens avidly promoted the adoption of stronger copyright laws in the United States. On his tour of the country in the 1840s, he was greeted as a hero of the common man until he complained about American booksellers routinely printing and selling his books without paying him royalties. The press criticized him but he exacted revenge with unflattering portraits of the United States in *American Notes and Martin Chuzzlewit*. *See* Sherri Burr, *The Piracy Gap: Protecting Intellectual Property in an Era of Artistic Creativity and Technological Change*, 33 WILLAMETTE L. REV. 245, 248 (1997).

Mark Twain also advocated the United States adopt more stringent copyright laws. He became upset after a boy tried to sell him a pirated version of *The Adventures of Tom Sawyer*. He sued several booksellers for printing his books in other countries and importing them into the United States. After one of his lawsuits failed, Twain wrote:

"A Massachusetts judge has just decided in open court that a Boston publisher may sell not only his own property in a free and

> unfettered way, but also may as freely sell property which does not belong to him, but to me—property which he has not bought and which I have not sold. Under this ruling, I am now advertising that the judge's homestead is for sale and if I make as good a sum out of it as I expect, I shall go out and sell the rest of his property."

Id. at 249. There is no evidence that Twain ever carried out his threat. It would take nearly a century before the United States joined the Berne Conviction, the major international copyright treaty designed to prevent the kind of theft that Dickens and Twain experienced on a grand scale.

The United States began to change its position on copyright piracy after it became a net exporter of intellectual property creations following World War II. Only then did legislators see the advantage to strengthening U.S. copyright laws. By the 1980s, the U.S. had become one of the principal providers of intellectual property to the rest of the world. Reagan Administration officials campaigned vigorously to have developing countries like China, Brazil, and Thailand curtail theft. The Reagan Administration came to view protecting intellectual property rights as critical to the continued growth of the U.S. economy.

The L.A. Times reported in 1993 that in Thailand, "pirates control 90% of the video market ... and reportedly cost the U.S. film industry about $30 million.... Total U.S. losses due to piracy in Thailand were about $123 million in 1992, including $49 million on computer programs and $20 million on books, according to industry officials." *International Trade Thai Piracy Likely to Top U.S. Hit List Property rights,* L.A. TIMES, Apr. 26, 1993, at D2.

More than a decade after the L.A. Times article ran, the problem with international theft of films, television shows, and music produced in the United States has expanded rather than contracted. Music piracy, for example, has reached a global epidemic, hitting countries as diverse as Italy and Egypt.

The International Federal Phonographic Industry (IFPI), whose 1500 members come from 76 countries, reported that in 2001, Italy placed sixth worldwide in terms of piracy valued at $121 million. Jay Berman, the chairman and CEO of IFPI, said, "Italy has a rich and vibrant musical culture, but the value of this music is being undermined by piracy on a massive scale.... [P]irate CDs are ... sold everywhere in the streets. Even when prosecutions do reach the courts, pirates often get off much too lightly." *See* www.ifpi.org/site-content/press/20030707.html.

In Egypt, the police seized nearly two million counterfeit Arab language music cassettes on July 7, 2003. The IFPI reported that next to Lebanon, where the piracy rate is almost 70%,

Egypt has one of the highest piracy rates in the Middle East region at about 50%. *Id.*

Technology has made it easier to steal with impunity. Films appear on the Internet the day of their release, sometimes with a laughter track that indicates they were surreptitiously taped in front of a theater audience. Other times, bootleg copies of movies become available for purchase before the film appears in the theatre.

Producers of the 2004 film *Soul Plane* blamed the bootleg copies for its poor performance at the box office. *See* Gabriel Snyder, *Was 'Plane' hijacked?,* June 8, 2004, *available at* http://www.variety.com/article/ VR1117906188?categoryid=13&cs=1. Gabriel Snyder wrote that the film "crashed with critics, but ... was a huge hit with bootleggers." *Id.*

Snyder noted that for years "in overseas markets, Hollywood has had to contend with bootleg copies of their films being sold on the street well before their theatrical release.... But this incident marks the earliest pirates have gotten hold of a major movie ahead of its U.S. release." *Id. Soul Plane* was available on the black market two months before it showed up in theaters.

Bootleggers enable their customers to avoid trips to the theater to see films or to stores to purchase copies. Ultimately, they may undermine production and creativity. *Soul Plane* cost $16 million to produce and recouped only

$13,957,242 during its 30-day box office run. When considering whether to do another film like *Soul Plane*, the producers must mull over whether they can keep the film under wraps long enough to recoup their investment.

If bootleggers aren't enough of a problem, on the horizon are computers so sophisticated that individuals will be able to download theater-quality films onto their personal systems for playback on home screens. With this level of theft occurring, the entertainment industry may be battling a beast that it cannot slay. As a consequence, many producers and studios seek to lower their production costs so they have higher profit margins to absorb losses from theft.

B. EXPANDING PRODUCTION VENUES

This section discusses the expanding nationalization and internationalization of film production. As producers seek to trim costs, they are generating films and television shows in places far beyond the traditional venues of California and New York. Several Hollywood producers and studios film in states that offer incentives to cut costs and many more go abroad to Canada, Europe, Australia, and other countries.

Globalization is a multi-lane highway. Foreign firms have purchased or engaged in deals with Hollywood studios to expand their reach into the United States. Sometimes foreigner's Hollywood adventures result in rude awakenings. Japanese conglomerate Sony bought Columbia studios and eventually had to fire the two Hollywood producers it put in charge to run their investment. While Peter Guber and Jon Peters had produced the mega hit *Batman*, they proved inept at running a studio. Nancy Griffin memorialized Sony's tale of woe in her book *Hit and Run: How Peter Guber and Jon Peters took Sony for a Ride in Hollywood*.

Given that Hollywood is in the fantasy business, some firms mistakenly expect studios to produce hit after hit. Yet as screenwriter William Goldman said in his *Adventures in the Screen Trade*, "Nobody Knows Anything." Goldman, *supra* note 2, at 39. In other words, the magic formula that produced a mega hit could easily produce 10 flops.

In 1996, German television giant, the Kirch Group, invested $2 billion in Universal Studios to lock up film and TV rights for its fledgling digital pay-TV systems, according to a Los Angeles Times article. Feeling duped after Universal released duds such as *Babe: Pig in the City* and *Meet Joe Black*, the Kirch Group sued Universal. *See Universal Sued by Kirch Over Film Quantity, Quality*, L.A. TIMES, Dec. 16, 1999, at C.1. While Universal did release hits such as *Notting Hill* and *The Mummy*, it also cut back on film production to contain spiraling costs. The Kirch Group expected Universal to provide 20 to 30 films and ended up with a fraction of that number. *Id.* The Kirch Group also expressed concern that Universal had shifted its attention from film and television production to music. *Id.*

By 2002, Universal sued the Kirch Group after it stopped payments on their 1996 deal. At that time, Universal's international television co-president Phil Schuman proclaimed, "We're the studio of the moment." Elizabeth Guider, *Mouse House springs passel of new deals*, VARIETY, Jan. 23, 2002, *available at* http://www.variety.com/index.asp?layout=natp e2002&content=story&nav=news&head=news& articleID=VR1117859055.

Hollywood is not the only film industry to produce illusory financial success. Variety Magazine reported, "At first glance, the bottom line on Australia's film industry is simple. While sales agents and other investors might turn small profits, fewer than 10% of films ever fully recoup their entire production budgets and go into overall profit.... Of the 110 or so films that the FFC [Film Finance Corp.] invested in through June 1997, about seven have gone into profit, including 'Sirens,' 'Green Card,' 'Shine,' 'Strictly Ballroom,' 'Priscilla,' and 'Muriel's Wedding'." *Oz Bottom Line Shaky* (Australian Film Industry), VARIETY MAG., Feb. 22, 1999, at xx.

To diminish the risk associated with film production and increase the potential for profit, Hollywood and foreign filmmakers cut production costs. They search out foreign and U.S. locales that offer tax incentives, which make films cheaper to create.

U.S. firms that produce films and television shows in foreign settings are sometimes termed runaway productions. A study released in 1999 estimated that the U.S. economy suffered a direct loss of $2.8 billion in 1998 from runaway productions. This was five times the 1990 figure of $500 million. *See* Sharon Waxman, *Location, Location; Hollywood Loses Films to Cheaper Climes*, WASH. POST, June 26, 1999. The study reported that of the 1,075 film and television productions released in the Untied Sates during 1998, 27 percent were produced abroad for economic reasons. *Id.* Eighty-one percent of these were filmed in Canada, whose government offers tax credits that can save 22% on labor costs. *Id.*

Canada is also a popular venue because its exchange rate against the U.S. dollar benefits Americans and because its cities can double for several American cities. For example, Toronto resembles New York, Chicago, and L.A., and it is cleaner than its American counterparts. Warner Brothers President of Production, Lorenzo di Bonaventura, said he was able to initially make *The Matrix* in 1999 for 30 percent less because the Canadian "rate of exchange is 62 cents on the dollar." *Id.*

Several other countries have followed Canada's lead by forming film commissions to solicit international entertainment dollars. In *How Foreign Film Commissions Can Lower Production Costs*, attorney Kevin Garrett Monroe discusses the advantages to filming in Hong Kong, Australia, Austria, France, Germany, Jamaica, Ireland, the Philippines and South Africa. Monroe notes, for example, that the government of Hong Kong budgeted $100 million for seminars and programs to train film and television professionals. Further, the Australian government funded a Film Bank with $80 million to foster its local film industry. It encourages foreigners to enter into co-production arrangements with Australians.

This co-production arrangement has many benefits as it increases production experience by partnering locals with foreigners. Monroe says the Austrian film commission maintains a list of Austrian producers who are qualified to enter into co-production arrangements. In return, Austria requires the foreigner to spend at least 300% of the funded amount in the country in filming costs, talent, hotel, and travel expenses. *Id.*

In adding these requirements, foreign film commissions are aiming for a multiplier effect to bring in a multiple of their expended investment into their communities. In the 1999 U.S. study on runaway productions, it estimated that the multiplier loss to the U.S. economy was $10.3

billion. Waxman, *supra*, at 313. This loss affected industries such as real estate, restaurants, clothing and hotels, and cost 20,000 jobs.

To stem this loss of revenue and jobs, some state legislatures have passed their own incentives. The New Mexico Investment Council, for example, invests up to $7.5 million, which may represent 100% of the budget of a film with an anticipated rating of "R" or lower. To qualify, according to Frank Zuniga, former director of the New Mexico Film Office, "The producer must (1) shoot their film wholly or substantially in the State of New Mexico; (2) must have a distribution agreement or pre-sales plan in place; (3) 60% of the below-the-line payroll must be New Mexico residents; (4) they must have a completion bond; and (5) have a guarantor that will guarantee payment of the loan." Burr and Henslee, *supra* note 1, at 206. Zuniga noted that New Mexico's money is never at risk due to the latter two requirements. As a result of these incentives, New Mexico went from having one or two films a year shot within its borders to one a month.

Florida and Miami-Dade County have also considered increasing incentives to encourage film production. According to Bill Dunlap, The Miami Dade Mayor's Office of Film & Entertainment doubled its marketing budget to $225,000. *See* Bill Dunlap, *Coping With Budget Blues: Film Offices Prove Their Worth*, SHOOT MAG. Jan. 24, 2003.

Not all states are inclined to hitch their economic resources to Hollywood bandwagons. While New Mexico increased its incentives, other states, like Arizona and Colorado, cut funding for their film commissions. Ohio and Wisconsin closed their film commission offices after developing budget woes. *Id.*

The globalization of the film and television industries creates an odd paradox for the U.S. economy. On the one hand, U.S. studios and producers benefit when they can make films cheaper. It increases their potential profit margin and permits them to absorb the loss associated with increased international and national piracy of their films. Yet, on the other hand, when studios produce abroad, they take jobs and revenue with them. It is for this reason that the New Mexico incentive plan has received a great deal of media intention as it permits studios and producers to cut their costs while keeping jobs and revenue within the United States.

C. INTERNATIONAL DISPUTE FORUMS

This section addresses issues associated with global dispute resolution. As studios and producers internationalize their operations, inevitably disputes arise with their foreign partners and other companies. Shopping for an appropriate forum to resolve the dispute becomes another source of concern.

In *London Films v. Intercontinental Communications*, 580 F.Supp. 47 (S.D.N.Y. 1984), a British corporation sued a New York Corporation for infringement of British copyrights that occurred in Chile and other South American countries. London Films alleged that Intercontinental was showing its motion pictures on television in South America. Intercontinental sought to dismiss the suit by claiming the court lacked jurisdiction. It expressed concern that none of the wrongdoings constitute violations of U.S. law.

While the court acknowledged that London Films did not allege that Intercontinental violated U.S. laws, the court determined that it possessed jurisdiction over whether an American corporation has acted in violation of a foreign copyright. The court noted that it was the only forum in which the defendant is the subject of personal jurisdiction. The court concluded that where "the balance does not tip strongly in favor of an alternative forum it is well-established that the plaintiff's choice of forum should not be disturbed." *Id.* at 50.

In some cases with individuals from different countries, courts endeavor to balance the private and public interest in deciding whether a plaintiff's choice of forum should be rejected on grounds of *forum non conveniens*. In *Overseas Programming Companies, Ltd. v. Cinematographische Commerz-Anstalt*, 684 F.2d 232, (2nd Cir. 1982), Judge Newman wrote that among a litigant's private interests to be considered are (1) the relative ease of access to sources of proof; (2) the availability of compulsory process for attendance of unwilling and cost of obtaining willing witnesses; and (3) other matters affecting the cost, speed, and ease of litigating a suit in a particular forum. *Id.* at 234.

Further, the judge observed that a court must also evaluate the enforceability of a judgment rendered by it; weigh relative advantages and obstacles to a fair trial; and determine whether the plaintiff has instituted suit in a particular forum with the intent to vex or harass the defendant. *Id.* The judge said the public interests to be considered include (1) the administrative burdens imposed on already congested courts by suits that are properly centered elsewhere and (2) the burden of jury duty on members of a community with no real relation to the dispute. *Id.* T he court applied these factors to reverse the district court and ordered that the case be tried in the United States because England was not a more convenient forum.

The Second Circuit applied similar factors and affirmed the dismissal of an action against the British Broadcasting Corporation on *forum non conveniens* grounds. In *Murray v. BBC*, 81, F.3d 287, (2nd Cir. 1996), both the plaintiff and the defendant were British nationals and the plaintiff asserted claims based on copyright infringement under both U.S. and English law.

Another important issue concerns whether the U.S. copyright laws can be extended extraterritorially to actions that take place in other countries. In *Subafilms, Ltd. v. MGM-Pathe Communications Co.*, 24 F.3d 1088 (9th Cir. 1994), the Ninth Circuit held that it lacked jurisdiction when the infringing conduct occurred abroad. The court noted that Congress has only declared that "the unauthorized importation of copyrighted works constitute infringement even when the copies lawfully were made abroad." *See* 17 U.S. C. § 602 (a) cited in Subafilms, 24 F.3d at 1096. The court said there is a presumption against the extraterritorial application of U.S. copyright Law, and thus United States copyright laws do not reach acts of infringement that take place entirely abroad. *Id.* at 1098. Indeed, to extend U.S. copyright laws would "disrupt the international regime for protecting intellectual property that Congress ... described as essential to ... protecting the works of American authors abroad." *Id.*

In *Richard Feiner v. BMG Music Spain*, 2003 WL 740605 (S.D.N.Y. 2003), the district court said an exception exists "where the defendant commits a predicate act of infringement within the U.S." BMG Music Spain produced compact disc recordings of the soundtrack from the movie *Marjorie Morningstar* in Spain and sold the discs in Europe. Feiner alleged that BMG Spain first copied a master copy of the recordings in the New York offices of co-defendant Bertelsmann Music Group, Inc., which it then used in Spain. There was also some question as to whether a portion of the Spanish production found its way into the United States. These were issues that the court felt should go to a jury to determine the extent of a U.S. connection to the infringing acts.

Courts are thus willing to take cases where there is a defined U.S. connection to the infringing acts. They are also unwilling to dismiss cases if it means that the plaintiff will not receive his day in court.

And with these words so comes the end to your journey through the legal maze that is Hollywood.

The End

Index

References are to Pages